Peak District
White Peak

Walks

Compiled by
Dennis and Jan Kelsall

Text: Dennis and Jan Kelsall
Photography: Dennis and Jan Kelsall
Editorial: Ark Creative (UK) Ltd
Design: Ark Creative (UK) Ltd

This product includes mapping data licensed from Ordnance Survey® with the permission of the Controller of Her Majesty's Stationery Office. © Crown Copyright 2009. All rights reserved. Licence number 150002047. Ordnance Survey, the OS symbol and Pathfinder are registered trademarks and Explorer, Landranger and Outdoor Leisure are trademarks of the Ordnance Survey, the national mapping agency of Great Britain.

ISBN 978-1-85458-495-3

While every care has been taken to ensure the accuracy of the route directions, the publishers cannot accept responsibility for errors or omissions, or for changes in details given. The countryside is not static: hedges and fences can be removed, field boundaries can alter, footpaths can be rerouted and changes in ownership can result in the closure or diversion of some concessionary paths. Also, paths that are easy and pleasant for walking in fine conditions may become slippery, muddy and difficult in wet weather, while stepping stones across rivers and streams may become impassable.

If you find an inaccuracy in either the text or maps, please write to Crimson Publishing at the address below.

First published in Great Britain 2009 by Crimson Publishing,
a division of:
Crimson Business Ltd,
Westminster House, Kew Road, Richmond, Surrey, TW9 2ND

www.totalwalking.co.uk

Printed in Singapore. 1/09

A catalogue record for this book is available from the British library.

Front cover: The path down to Goytsclough Quarries
Previous page: The heath above the head of Black Brook

Contents

Safety on the Hills;
Walkers and the Law;
Countryside Access Charter;
Useful Organisations;
Ordnance Survey Maps

Approximate walk times

 Up to 2½ hours   3–3½ hours   4 hours and over

The walk times are provided as a guide only and are calculated using an average walking speed of 2½mph (4km/h), adding one minute for each 10m (33ft) of ascent, and then rounding the result to the nearest half hour.

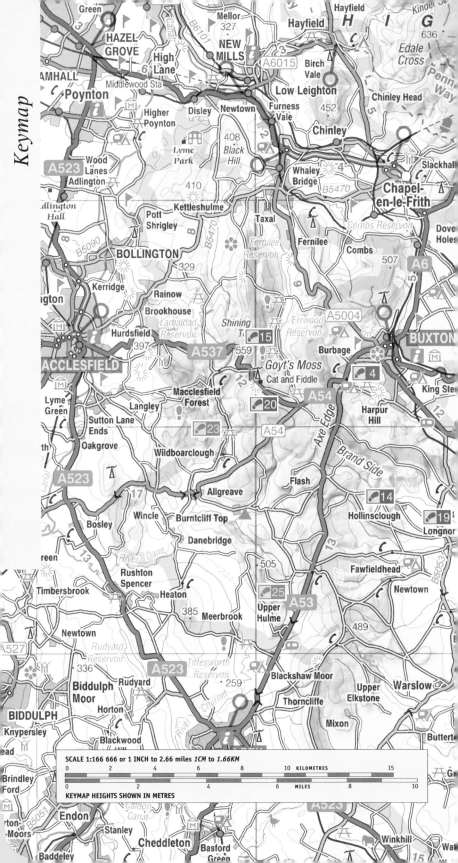

Keymap

P E A K

590
318
A57
10

Edale
River Noe
Ladybower Reservoir
463
High Neb
458
Redmires Reservoirs
Fulw

ber
oth
518
Tumuli
Hope
Aston
A6013
Bamford
457

Castleton
Thornhill
Hathersage
Fort
12
T

Peveril Castle
Brough
A6187

470
427
417
B6049
A6187
7

23
Peak Forest
Coplow Dale
Abney
Stone Circle
Owler Bar

PEAK
Little Hucklow
Great Hucklow
Grindleford
Nether Padley
B6054

NATIONAL PARK
Grindlow
429
367
A621

Wheston
Foolow
17
Eyam
26
Eyam Hall
Froggatt
305

Tideswell
Litton
Stoney Middleton
A625

06
17
Wardlow
Calver
Curbar

Wormhill
Miller's Dale
6
Cressbrook
B6465
A623
21

10
Little Longstone
Rowland
Baslow
Robin H

8
Blackwell
River Wye
Great Longstone
Hassop
Pilsley
Robin

A5270
Monsal Head
A6020
Chatsworth House
East

Taddington
Chelmorton
5
Ashford in the Water
11
A619
Edensor
B6012

Sheldon
355
BAKEWELL
27
Beeley
13

Flagg
B5055
Over Haddon
A6
Haddon Hall
Rowsley

A515
28
Monyash
Alport
Stanton in Peak
Northwood

owdicote
ROMAN ROAD
Arbor Low
Youlgrave
Middleton
B5056
Stone
C
River Derwent
Darley Dale

Pilsbury
Pennine Bridleway
Birchover
1
Two Dales

380
9
380
Elton
330
Darley Bridge
B5057
Upper Hackney

Hartington
2
Winster
Wens
3

B5054
22
te
Diggin
Pikehall
A5012
Brightgate
Bonsall
MATLOCK
Rib

Hulme End
388
382
Aldwark
10
Grangemill
Matlock Bath
Derw

Alstonefield
Longcliffe
Ible
Middleton
B5023
Cromfo

etton
16
A515
Alsop en le Dale
Ballidon
Brassington
18
Bolehil

Hopedale
Milldale
Parwich
WIRKSWORTH
Whats

River Manifold
River Dove
Tissington Hall
Bradbourne
Carsington
Hopton
Alderwas

369
10
Tissington
B5056
Carsington Water
28

ilam
24
Fenny
Thorpe
B5035

Walk	Page	Start	Nat. Grid Reference	Distance	Time	Height Gain
A Five Dales Walk	53	Tideswell	SK 152757	6¾ miles (10.9km)	3½ hrs	1,250ft (381m)
Ashford in the Water and Monsal Dale	35	Ashford in the Water	SK 194697	6 miles (9.7km)	3 hrs	1,130ft (344m)
Bakewell, Chatsworth Park and the River Wye	84	Bakewell	SK 219684	10½ miles (16.9km)	5 hrs	1,290ft (393m)
Baslow and Curbar edges	65	Baslow	SK 258722	7¼ miles (11.7km)	3½ hrs	1,140ft (347m)
Beeley and Hob Hurst's House	41	Beeley	SK 265674	6¼ miles (10.1km)	3 hrs	950ft (290m)
Beresford and Wolfscote dales	68	Hartington	SK 128604	8 miles (12.9km)	4 hrs	1,360ft (415m)
Brand Side and the Source of the Dove	44	Hollinsclough	SK 065664	6½ miles (10.5km)	3 hrs	1,230ft (375m)
Chee Dale	32	Miller's Dale	SK 138732	5¾ miles (9.3km)	3 hrs	1,290ft (393m)
Chelmorton to Deep Dale	26	Wye Dale	SK 103724	5¼ miles (8.4km)	2½ hrs	810ft (247m)
Chrome Hill	59	Longnor	SK 088649	7 miles (11.3km)	3½ hrs	1,500ft (457m)
Cromford and Matlock Bath	56	Cromford Wharf	SK 299570	7 miles (11.3km)	3½ hrs	1,390ft (424m)
Deep Dale and the Magpie Mine	20	White Lodge	SK 170705	4¾ miles (7.6km)	2½ hrs	780ft (238m)
Eyam, Bretton Clough and Eyam Moor	80	Eyam	SK 216767	9¼ miles (14.9km)	4½ hrs	1,620ft (494m)
Grin Low and Buxton Country Park	18	Grin Low and Buxton Country Park	SK 049719	4½ miles (7.2km)	2 hrs	620ft (189m)
Heights of Abraham and Bonsall	16	Matlock Bridge Park	SK 298601	4¼ miles (6.8km)	2 hrs	1,060ft (323m)
Ilam and Dovedale	74	Dovedale	SK 146509	8 miles (12.9km)	4 hrs	1,660ft (506m)
Lathkill Dale	88	Monyash	SK 149666	10½ miles (16.9km)	5 hrs	1,600ft (488m)
Longshaw and Padley Gorge	24	Longshaw Country Park	SK 266800	5 miles (8km)	2½ hrs	840ft (256m)
Macclesfield Forest & the 'Cheshire Matterhorn'	71	Wildboarclough	SJ 986699	7¾ miles (12.5km)	4 hrs	1,770ft (540m)
Pilsbury Castle	29	Hartington	SK 128604	5½ miles (8.9km)	2½ hrs	830ft (253m)
Stanton Moor	12	Birchover, by The Druid Inn	SK 236621	3 miles (4.8km)	1½ hrs	470ft (143m)
The Goyt Valley and Shining Tor	47	Errwood Reservoir	SK 012748	6½ miles (10.5km)	3½ hrs	1,310ft (399m)
The Manifold Valley	50	Wetton	SK 109551	6½ miles (10.5km)	3½ hrs	1,420ft (433m)
The Roaches and Lud's Church	77	Roaches Gate	SK 004621	8¼ miles (13.3km)	4 hrs	1,420ft (433m)
Three Shire Heads and Axe Edge Moor	62	Cat and Fiddle Inn	SK 000718	7¼ miles (11.7km)	3½ hrs	1,080ft (329m)
Tissington and Alsop en le Dale	38	Tissington	SK 178520	6¼ miles (10.1km)	3 hrs	820ft (250m)
Winster and Birchover	14	Winster	SK 238602	4 miles (6.4km)	2 hrs	750ft (229m)
Wormhill and Monk's Dale	22	Miller's Dale	SK 138732	4¾ miles (7.6km)	2½ hrs	920ft (280m)

Comments

Five dales in a day, with every one different. The walk sets out from the lively village of Tideswell, whose grand church is known as the 'Cathedral of the Peak'.

The superb viewpoint of Monsal Head serves as a dramatic prelude to this grand promenade of Monsal Dale and the River Wye.

The neighbouring stately houses of Chatsworth and Haddon are both encountered on this exploration of the rolling countryside that rises to the east of Bakewell.

Gritstone edges feature in the south of the Peak District as well as the north and this route takes in two of the most dramatic before dropping to the banks of the River Derwent.

The goblins or hobs of local folklore inhabited mysterious settings, the one here being an unusual Bronze Age burial on the moor above the Chatsworth Estate.

The River Dove's succession of limestone gorges begins with Beresford and Wolfscote dales, which inspired Charles Cotton's contribution to his friend, Izaac Walton's fishing treatise, *The Compleat Angler*.

From the moors of Axe Edge, the River Dove cuts a rugged landscape of rounded hills and winding valleys, a fascinating contrast to the limestone gorges found lower down.

The narrow confines of beautiful Chee Dale leave no room for a footpath and the way through resorts to stepping stones along the bed of the stream.

The great beauty of the White Peak lies within its dales and Deep Dale is no exception with moss-draped woodland and steep wildflower meadows rising to rocky crags above.

This adventurous walk from the old market village of Longnor takes in the White Peak's most spectacular hills and traverses a sharp ridge known as the 'Dragon's Back'.

A Victorian spa, an early purpose-built town of the Industrial Revolution, a superb viewpoint and a picturesque canal are all featured in this day out from Cromford.

Magpie Mine's tall chimneys, a great ruined engine house and pit-head gear vividly illustrate the importance of the Peak's mine workings.

Contrasting landscapes of limestone plateau and gritstone heath are brought together on this walk beginning from Eyam, whose story of courage in the face of plague is told in the local museum.

The walk centres on the pastures and woodlands of Buxton Country Park, leaving time to visit the area's great show cave, Poole's Cavern.

The Heights of Abraham, famed for its views across Matlock's Derwent Gorge, and an attractive village with market cross and pub are features here.

The final section of the Dovedale gorge above the River Manifold is undoubtedly the most popular, and revels in spectacular scenery every single step of the way.

The open vistas of limestone plateau contrast with intimate scenes in the narrow gorge below on this day-long ramble through ever popular Lathkill Dale.

Scenic and historic interest on this walk from the former hunting lodge of the Duke of Rutland abounds, but the undoubted highlight is the lovely Padley Gorge.

Distant views from the north reveal Shutlingsloe as a worthy 'Cheshire Matterhorn', a satisfying objective of this wandering circuit within the ancient royal hunting domain of Macclesfield Forest.

Despite the lack of turreted battlements and vaulted undercrofts, Pilsbury is a spectacular castle site, reached here from the attractive former market town of Hartington.

Gritstone outcrops and prehistoric remains abound on Stanton Moor, competing for your attention with fine views over the Derwent Valley.

Shining Tor is the highest of the south Peak's hills, reached here along its northern ridge to reveal an unrivalled prospect over the Goyt Valley and surrounding countryside.

Among the features here are the disused trackbed of the former Manifold railway line, an old corn mill and a gaping cave high on the hillside.

The long edge of the Roaches and Back Forest offer one of the finest ridge walks in the south Peak, a succession of gritstone outcrops backed by a quiet moorland valley.

From the remote Cat and Fiddle Inn, this wild and wonderful ramble encircles moorland heads of the White Peak's major rivers, following the Dane to a pretty waterfall known as Three Shire Heads.

A section of the Tissington Trail, a disused railway track that ran between Buxton and Ashbourne, here links two of the Peak's most picturesque villages.

Winster's ancient market house and picturesque streets and alleyways provide a fitting end to this countryside foray to neighbouring Birchover.

Monk's Dale Nature Reserve harbours wild flowers, birds and insects, while Miller's Dale reveals the 19th-century limestone industry instigated by the railways.

At-a-glance...

Introduction to the Peak District

The area known as the Peak encompasses the southern extremity of the Pennine uplift, the longest contiguous range of hills in the country, which runs from the Scottish borders all the way to the Midland plains. Much of the Peak falls within Derbyshire, but the hills over-spill into the counties of Yorkshire, Staffordshire, Cheshire and Greater Manchester too. Despite a relatively compact size, barely 40 miles (64km) from top to bottom and only 20 miles (32km) wide, it embodies vividly contrasting landscapes, their disparate characters springing from the bedrock upon which they lie. The highest land is to be found in the north and is footed on gritstone, a hard impermeable sandstone that weathers almost to black. It gives rise to vast rolling moors abruptly bounded by dark, dramatically weatherworn cliffs known as 'edges'. Farther south, the gritstone runs out in two peripheral horns that embrace a lower, grassy limestone plateau, neatly partitioned by miles of drystone walls and riven by pretty dales and deep gorges, which grace the area with much of its beauty.

The word 'peak' might conjure an image of dramatic pinnacles and lofty heights, perhaps attained only after the effort of a scramble. But here you will find few craggy summits or prodigious heights, the greatest elevation of 2,088 feet (636m) being barely distinguishable amid an unrelieved wilderness on the Kinder plateau. 'Peak' in fact derives from the Old English word paec, meaning merely a hill, and the Anglo-Saxon peoples who settled here after the Romans abandoned Britain in the 5th century became known as the Pecsætna or Peak Dwellers. The name stuck and today describes one of the most popular regions for outdoor activity in the country.

The National Park

Despite the lack of 'peaks', this is grand walking country and was appreciated as such long before the National Park came into existence. By the close of the 19th century, industrial expansion was pushing at the edge of the moors and many factory workers looked to the clear, open spaces on their doorstep for recreation; a chance to escape the crowding, noise and dirt of their workaday lives. However, most of the land was private, preserved as grouse moors, sheep runs or water catchment for the numerous reservoirs being built in the higher valleys. Many viewed this blanket prohibition as a deep injustice and braved the often-aggressive gamekeepers to practise the 'gentle art of trespass'. Ramblers' groups and footpath preservation societies achieved some success in opening Rights of Way, yet the Kinder Trespass in 1932 was a milestone. Although neither the first nor the last mass trespass, it became iconic, partly because of its scale, some 500 people took to the moor, but also for the harshness of punishment meted out to the handful of ringleaders arrested. This turned the tide of public sympathy and developed a will to change the law, which eventually led to the enactment of the National Park and Access to the Countryside Act in 1949 and subsequently, the *Countryside and Rights of Way Act in 2000.*

The Peak District National Park was created in 1951 as a direct result of the 1949 Act, the first of its kind in Britain.

The White Peak

The great dome of Carboniferous limestone that rises south of Castleton gives the White Peak its name, a high, undulating plateau fractured by a web of deep gorges that radiate from its heart. It is in these depths that its most spectacular scenery is to be found; along the valleys of the River Dove, Manifold, Derwent, Wye and Lathkill and their innumerable tributaries. But this is karst country and in many places the river flows deep beneath the

Descending towards Goyt's Clough

ground leaving some dales completely dry and in others the water flowing only intermittently, mysteriously disappearing among the boulders to bubble up lower down as a sparkling spring. Such a landscape is riddled with caves and they are to be found in plenty, sometimes little more than a hollow going back only a few feet, but elsewhere, such as at Thor's Cave, a great, gaping yawn in the cliff. Most are inaccessible or the province of pot-holers, but a small number have been opened as show caves, such as those around Castleton and Poole's Cavern at Buxton.

Not all the subterranean holes are due to nature, for the Peak's limestone is richly veined in metal ores, in particular lead and copper. The ragged craters and hummocks of bell-pit mines can be found throughout the limestone area, often running in scabrous lines across a hillside following the outcropping seam. After the Romans left Britain until the dawn of the Industrial Revolution, these small mines provided farmers and their labourers with another source of income to supplement that derived from the thin soils of the farms. The development of steam engines, however, enabled the exploitation of deeper reserves, but in most mines, underground water was an ever-present and costly problem and falling lead prices and foreign competition meant that most mines had become uneconomic by the beginning of the 20th century. In one or two places, the full extent of the industry is vividly revealed, most notably in the lead museum and mines at

Introduction

Matlock and the substantial pit-head ruins of the Magpie Mine near Sheldon.

The limestone itself has also been extensively quarried over the centuries, originally on a small scale for local building and agricultural lime kilns, but the development of the railways racked up the scale of operations, literally moving mountains as vast industrial quarries opened. Some of these continue today and are a reason for the exclusion of the area around Buxton from the National Park.

Much of the countryside is given over to livestock and dairy farming; cattle grazing where the grass is richest and sheep roaming elsewhere. The fields and meadows of the plateau are partitioned within thousands of miles of drystone walls and sparsely dotted with barns, many of which were constructed during the 18th and 19th centuries although to most people they are timeless. Enclosed clumps of trees break the skyline, but they are often few and far between, the most extensive patches of rambling woodland being found in the bottoms of the dales. Predominantly of ash and thorn they harbour a rich and varied plant life supporting a population of small mammals, birds and other wildlife. In spring and early summer the understorey is rich in flowers, as are the uncultivated meadows and grasslands that rear up the steep valley sides. Some, like sections of Dovedale and the Manifold are justifiably well known for their outstanding beauty, but others, less often visited, have equally endearing qualities. Such habitats are now relatively rare in this country and Monk's Dale, Lathkill Dale and Deep Dale are among the many now protected as nature reserves.

Yet, the southern part of the Peak equally owes its character to the gritstone that bounds its flanks. As with the land to the north, the most dramatic features lie on the tors and along the upturned edges, where the ground falls precipitously from weatherworn cliffs to chaotic aprons of great boulders, sculpted into enigmatic and mystical shapes by millennia of frost and wind. The upper moors are less elevated than their northern counterparts and heath is more predominant than wilderness tracts of wet bog. Even so, the best walking is often to be found along the edges such as at Curbar, Baslow and the Roches, from which there are unrivalled views. The lower slopes are frequently clad in a luxuriant woodland of oak, birch and pine and, like their counterparts in the limestone dales, are home to many species of plants, animals, birds and insects. The rich woodlands of the Dane and Goyt valleys immediately spring to mind, but on the eastern flank, a trip to Padley Gorge is not to be missed.

The walks

Few places are remote from a small village or the web of narrow lanes and tracks that extend across the White Peak and general navigation is not a significant problem. However, countryside walking often demands attention to detail; being on the wrong side of a wall can usher you in the wrong direction, and the location of stiles and gates is essential in charting a course across a chequer-board of fields. Much of this part of the Peak is actively farmed and, away from the moors, as there are fewer swathes of open access land, it is important to follow recognised paths. *Several walks explore the higher ground of the region, which, like all hill areas, is susceptible to changeable weather and demands adequate equipment and experience.* Even in the sheltered dales, walking can be demanding for although climbs and descents may be relatively short, they are often abrupt. In the most popular gorges, good paths have been laid, but *elsewhere the terrain is often rocky and, in wet conditions, limestone polished by the passage of innumerable feet and steep grass slopes can become very slippery.*

In an area where there is so much worthy of exploration, the difficulty is not in what to include, but rather what to leave out. This collection has been chosen to explore the many different aspects of the countryside and sometimes include or lie close to another attraction. Among the notable things to see are Chatsworth House and Haddon Hall as well as many museums such as the lead museum at Matlock Bath and that relating the harrowing story of 17th-century plague in Eyam. Most villages have an interesting church, and although sadly many are locked, it is often possible to locate the keyholder. In a region where almost every village has character that invites exploration there are surprises, like the many-stepped cross at Bonsall and the narrow alleys at Winster.

The Park Authority does an excellent job in maintaining paths, stiles and gates. Together with canal towpaths, former railway lines, old tracks and quiet lanes, they offer endless possibilities for superb walking. There is an on-going policy to replace stiles with gates in popular areas, but you can expect to encounter stiles and squeeze gaps on every walk. In most places, well-behaved dogs are welcome and ought to be kept on leads near livestock, in farmyard areas and while passing through nature reserves. They should also be restrained during the spring nesting season upon the moor and note also that, in some open access areas, dogs are not permitted other than on Rights of Way. Welcoming country pubs and village cafés appear on or near many of the walks, but if you intend relying on them for something to eat, it is as well to check in advance that they will be open when you pass. Having said all that, all that remains is for you to choose your walk and set off.

This book includes a list of waypoints alongside the description of the walk, so that you can enjoy the full benefits of gps should you wish to. For more information on using your gps, read the *Pathfinder® Guide GPS for Walkers*, by gps teacher and navigation trainer, Clive Thomas (ISBN 978-0-7117-4445-5). For essential information on map reading and basic navigation, read the *Pathfinder® Guide Map Reading Skills* by outdoor writer, Terry Marsh (ISBN 978-0-7117-4978-8). Both titles are available in bookshops or can be ordered online at www.totalwalking.co.uk

Stanton Moor

		GPS waypoints
Start	Birchover, by The Druid Inn	
Distance	3 miles (4.8km)	SK 236 621
Height gain	470 feet (143m)	Ⓐ SK 241 628
Approximate time	1½ hours	Ⓑ SK 249 635
Parking	Roadside parking in Lower Village or parking area opposite Birchover Quarry on Birchover Road	Ⓒ SK 246 625
		Ⓓ SK 244 622
Route terrain	Heath and field paths	
Ordnance Survey maps	Landranger 119 (Buxton & Matlock), Explorer OL24 (The Peak District – White Peak area)	

Stanton Moor, a finger of gritstone amid limestone country, rises to 1,060 feet (323m) and is an open, breezy, heather-clad moorland giving glorious views across the valley of the Derwent. Its two chief characteristics, which form the main features of this short walk, are the curious rock formations and the vast number of prehistoric remains – burial chambers, standing stones, circles and fortifications – that litter the moor.

Birchover is a small village strung out along the hill that climbs to Stanton Moor. At its lower end, behind **The Druid Inn**, a path leads to the Rowtor Rocks, a gritstone outcrop worth exploring after the walk, both for its extensive views and its maze of caves and passages, where carved steps lead to staggered terraces. Many of these were the work of Thomas Eyre, an eccentric 18th-century clergyman, who also built, just beneath the rocks, the tiny village church.

🔖 The walk begins through a broad gap in the wall opposite **The Druid Inn**. A path climbs away between the trees, passing old quarries to emerge in a parking area at the top. Walk through to the road beyond and turn left. Follow it up the hill for ¼ mile, passing Birchover Quarry to find a marked footpath leaving on the right

Thomas Eyre's sanctuary

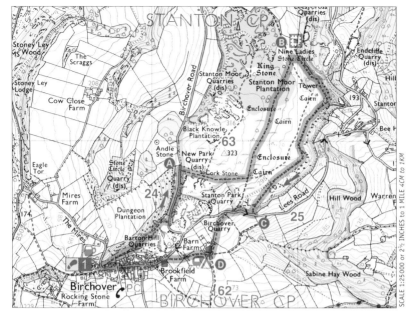

onto Stanton Moor .

Head through the trees to a stile and continue onto the moor, shortly reaching the Cork Stone, an isolated monolith on your left by a disused quarry. Bear right at the fork and keep going until you meet an obvious crossing of broad paths. Turn left and climb over open heather heath, where there are some fine views to the right across the Derwent Valley. After passing into birch woodland, look for the Nine Ladies Stone Circle in a clearing to the left, the most imposing of the many prehistoric remains that dot the moor. According to legend the ladies were turned to stone as punishment for dancing on the Sabbath. However, more prosaically the monument is thought to date from the Bronze Age and was probably erected around 1500BC. Like all such circles, nothing is really known about it, although it is presumed to have had some religious significance.

Walk a few yards beyond the circle and take a path off to the right , following it through trees to a stile. Over that, turn right beside the fence

above a steep escarpment, shortly passing the Reform Tower, erected in honour of Earl Grey, of Reform Bill (and blend of tea) fame. A little farther on, the path leads to a curious outcrop dubbed the Cat Stone, immediately before which, the path abruptly swings right. Keep going at the edge of the moor, passing more outcrops and eventually dropping to meet a lane .

Turn right, but after some 200 yds, abandon the lane for a waymarked footpath on the left. Carry on at the field edge to a farm at the bottom, skirting left around the buildings to pick up a track swinging right and signed to Winster. Stick with that only as far as a gate at the end of the buildings, leaving just beyond it over a squeeze stile on the right . Walk on by a fence to join a track from the farm that leads out to a lane. Follow it left downhill into the village, passing Birchover's other pub, **The Red Lion**, before returning to **The Druid Inn**. ●

Winster and Birchover

Start	Winster – car park off B5056 near Wyns Tor	GPS waypoints
		✏ SK 238 602
Distance	4 miles (6.4km)	Ⓐ SK 236 600
Height gain	750 feet (229m)	Ⓑ SK 228 615
Approximate time	2 hours	Ⓒ SK 236 621
Parking	At start	Ⓓ SK 240 621
Route terrain	Field paths and tracks	Ⓔ SK 243 617
Ordnance Survey maps	Landranger 119 (Buxton & Matlock), Explorer OL24 (The Peak District – White Peak area)	

Winster overlooks the geological boundary where limestone meets grit, each bestowing character upon the old buildings that line its streets. The walk passes between the two landscapes, crossing the broad valley to neighbouring Birchover and giving fine views across an open landscape.

✏ Walk from the car park to the main road, going left and then right onto a minor lane. After 200 yds, at a junction, take the track on the right signed as the Limestone Way Ⓐ. Keep right at a subsequent fork and then cross the drive to Westhill Farm. Emerging at a junction, the route continues along Dudwood Lane opposite, following it down the hill for over ¼ mile. Towards the bottom, turn off right, immediately beyond some cottages Ⓑ.

Pass through a gravel yard and a small field to emerge between trees at the far side onto the main road. Through a squeeze gate opposite, drop to a stream and head up at the edge of the field beyond. Leave to the left of a small barn at the top along a green track. Ignore a junction, but when you later meet the sharp bend of a stone track, take the lower branch. It dips beside the old vicarage and up past the church. Rowtor Rocks, (*referred to in Walk 1)*, are to be found along a path

on the left, immediately before **The Druid Inn** and are well worth exploring.

Founded on gritstone, Birchover's industry revolved around quarrying and the warm-coloured sandstone that faces most of the village's buildings is still cut today. The quarries were famed for their millstones, which were exported around the world.

Turn right by **The Druid Inn** Ⓒ along the main street, passing Upper Town Lane before leaving just beyond the Wesleyan chapel for a track on the right signed as a footpath Ⓓ. Wind between buildings to a yard, from which a gate leads to the field behind. Walk away, continuing along a narrow field, to find a small gate slightly left in the end boundary. Carry on at the field edge, but then, passing into the next field, go right, leaving through a gate at the corner, soon reaching a track, Clough Lane Ⓔ.

Through another gate opposite, follow a grass track over a rise, staying with the left boundary down to a stile into Stoop Wood. The ongoing path drops steeply through the trees, continuing beyond across a succession of rough pastures towards Winster. A flagged causeway avoids the marsh surrounding emergent springs and climbs to a back street that leads into the centre of the village.

The Portway has brought passing trade since the Bronze Age, but Winster's expansion came in the 1600s with the exploitation of rich veins of lead ore threading the limestone hills upon whose flanks the village clings. The curious Market House, now cared for by the National Trust, reflects that prosperity.

Turn right in front of the Market House, climbing past **The Old Bowling Green**, one of the village's two pubs to a fork. Keep right as far as Orchard Lime Cottage, there going left and then right up a stepped path to the top of the village. The car park can be found a short distance along the lane to the right. ●

Henry Tomkins was a hawker, dealt in small wares and made pattens and clogs

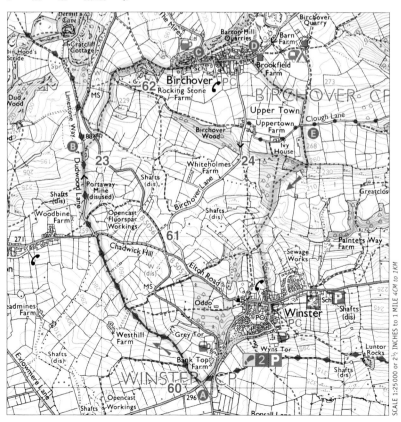

Heights of Abraham and Bonsall

Start	Matlock Bridge Park	**GPS waypoints**	
Distance	4¼ miles (6.8km)		SK 298 601
Height gain	1,060 feet (323m)	**Ⓐ**	SK 294 599
		Ⓑ	SK 293 592
Approximate time	2 hours	**Ⓒ**	SK 291 587
Parking	In town	**Ⓓ**	SK 279 583
Route terrain	Woodland and field paths and tracks	**Ⓔ**	SK 279 590
Ordnance Survey maps	Landranger 119 (Buxton & Matlock), Explorer OL24 (The Peak District – White Peak area)		

Beginning from Matlock Bridge, upstream of the spa, the walk climbs from the gorge to the former lead-mining village of Bonsall. The return follows old tracks across the high ground, which peers up the Derwent Valley towards the Chatsworth lands.

Leaving the riverside park, cross Matlock Bridge and keep ahead up Snitterton Road. Beyond a right-hand bend branch left on a track to Bridge Farm. Walk past the front of the farmhouse to the field behind and climb to a squeeze stile at the top **Ⓐ**. Follow a track left towards Matlock Bath, but approaching a bend before Greenhills Farm, leave beside a gate on the left from

which a twisting grass path undulates across hillside meadow. Entering woodland continue below Shining Cliff. Later meeting a narrow track, head up the hill. At the top look for a path on the right signed to the Heights of Abraham **Ⓑ**. Climb steeply beside a wall, passing through a gap before emerging from woodland onto a more open hillside. A superb view opens across the valley to the Victorian gothic Riber Castle and the cliffs below High Tor.

A trod guides you across the hillside then turns once more to face the gradient, rising through scrub towards a round tower, the Heights of Abraham. Reaching a side entrance to the complex **Ⓒ**, ignore the gate and follow the wall up to a collapsed stile. Walk above the boundary, crossing the

Bonsall's market square and cross

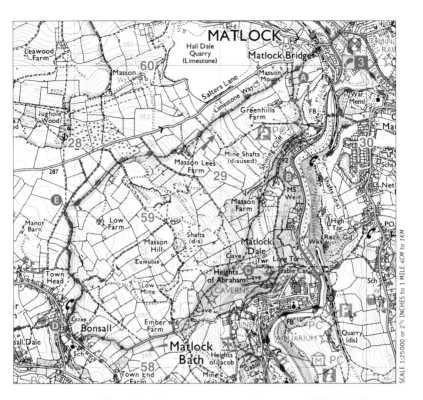

SCALE 1:25 000 or 2½ INCHES to 1 MILE 4CM to 1KM

```
0    200   400   600  800 METRES  1
                                  KILOMETRES
                                  MILES
0    200   400   600 YARDS  ½
```

main entrance drive and continue through woodland beyond.

Emerging from the trees onto a rough field track, go right through a gate and turn left to follow a track from Ember Farm. After cresting the hill, it winds down between leafy walls to Bonsall, ending opposite St James Church. Go right, but then branch right along a narrow alleyway to emerge above the square, dominated by a stepped market cross **D**.

Turn right along a restricted byway that climbs determinedly from the village. At a fork, go left, beyond which the gradient eases. Reaching another junction turn right for another short climb, looking for a dilapidated signpost and broken stile on the right near the crest of the hill **E**.

Head across to the end of a wall by a power cable post and follow it left past a barn. Continue across the next field to a track. Through a stile opposite, cut right to another stile and go left on the other flank of the wall, which guides you down a scrubby hillside to a kissing-gate. Passing out onto a track, walk right, but then leave after a few yards by a signpost on the left. Head down the edge of the field and across a smaller paddock to come out by the entrance to Masson Lees Farm. Opposite, the ongoing path descends more fields, shortly encountering a field track beneath overhead power cables. Slip through a gate and carry on down the hill with the hedge on your right. A trod guides you across successive enclosures, eventually reaching a wooden stile beyond which the path forks. Choose the right branch through scrub to emerge onto a track at Point **A**. The way back lies along your outward path through the stile opposite. ●

Grin Low and Buxton Country Park

		GPS waypoints
Start	Grin Low and Buxton Country Park	🖉 SK 049 719
Distance	4½ miles (7.2km)	Ⓐ SK 054 717
Height gain	620 feet (189m)	Ⓑ SK 050 724
Approximate time	2 hours	Ⓒ SK 054 724
Parking	Car park at start (Pay and Display)	Ⓓ SK 058 712
Route terrain	Farm tracks, field and woodland paths	Ⓔ SK 043 718
Ordnance Survey maps	Landranger 119 (Buxton & Matlock), Explorer OL24 (The Peak District – White Peak area)	

Buxton Country Park is centred on Grin Low Woods, a landscape once blighted by quarrying and lime burning. The short ramble takes in Solomon's Temple, a 19th-century folly and fine viewpoint and continues across the neighbouring hills, but allows plenty of time to visit the impressive show cave of Poole's Cavern.

Buxton is the Peak District's answer to Bath or Cheltenham – an elegant spa town with some fine buildings. Most notable are the 18th-century Crescent, the Devonshire Hospital, the Regency church, the Victorian Pavilion and gardens and the opulent Edwardian Opera House.

🖉 From the car park, a well-surfaced path signed to Poole's Cavern and Solomon's Temple climbs from the quarry. Meeting another path go left and then, at a second junction swing right through a gate. Walk on, initially beside Grin Low Woods before striking out to the folly, which breaks the skyline ahead Ⓐ. Solomon's Temple, otherwise known as Grinlow Tower, was built in 1896 by Solomon Mycock to provide work for the unemployed. From the top you can look out to Mam Tor and Kinder Scout. Heading north towards the town, mount a wall stile and continue down to a broken wall. Go left, crossing a stile beside a gate into Grin Low Woods, which were planted by the sixth Duke of Devonshire in 1820 to hide the devastation of old lime pits. Walk ahead through the trees, ignoring

Looking from Stanley Moor to Grin Low

side paths until you reach an obvious T-junction. To the right, the way descends the hillside, eventually reaching a stepped path that drops right to Poole's Cavern car park **B**. An impressive natural cave, it yielded Roman artefacts and takes its name from a medieval outlaw who reputedly used it as his lair.

Cross the car park to a gate opposite from which a path leads past a derelict building to the road. Walk right for 250 yds before turning off through the gated entrance to Buxton Community School Playing Fields **C**. Bear left along the perimeter to a shallow corner, there passing through the hedge to join an enclosed path. Follow it right, emerging into a field at its end and carry on beside the right-hand edge, meeting a rough lane in front of houses. Walk right, but after a cattle-grid, leave to cross a stile to the right. Turn left along the field edge towards Fern House Farm, mounting a stile and continuing

on a contained way beside successive paddocks. Reaching the stables, dogleg around an equestrian exercise enclosure, leaving beyond it along a rising track at the edge of a wood. Entering a field at the top, carry on in the same direction to a stile in the far corner. Keep going downhill, bearing right to cross a field track before reaching Grin Low Road over a final stile **D**.

Go left and then leave right, crossing a stile beside a gate to follow a track over a stream before winding uphill to a farm. Entering the yard, turn immediately right through a gate. Skirt the buildings to emerge onto a track. Heading from the farm, it meanders across the valley and later below Stanley Moor Reservoir, offering superb views to Axe Edge.

Reaching the road **E**, cross to the country park and follow the drive back to the car park. The open ground has been reclaimed from old workings, whilst the main quarry was converted into an attractive campsite for the Caravan Club of Great Britain in 1981–2. ●

```
0    200   400   600   800 METRES  1
                                    KILOMETRES
                                    MILES
0    200   400   600 YARDS  1/2
```

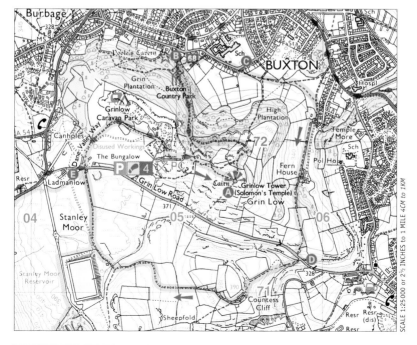

SCALE 1:25000 or 2½ INCHES to 1 MILE 4CM to 1KM

Deep Dale and the Magpie Mine

		GPS waypoints
Start	White Lodge at foot of Taddington Dale	SK 170 705
Distance	4¾ miles (7.6km)	**A** SK 169 702
Height gain	780 feet (238m)	**B** SK 158 685
Approximate time	2½ hours	**C** SK 166 681
Parking	Car park beside A6 at start (Pay and Display)	**D** SK 172 681
		E SK 173 687
Route terrain	Field paths, tracks, steep descent	**F** SK 173 692
		G SK 169 695
Ordnance Survey maps	Landranger 119 (Buxton & Matlock), Explorer OL24 (The Peak District – White Peak area)	

One of several Deep Dales, this climbs from the Wye Valley onto the limestone plateau. The area was heavily mined for lead and the walk leads past one of the best-preserved mines in the country. Open views accompany the return from Sheldon, which concludes in a steep descent at the edge of Great Shacklow Wood.

Follow a path from the payment machine across the adjoining picnic area to a gate. Carry on over another meadow, ignoring a path off to Taddington to meet a stream. Follow it up a short distance, crossing to a stile. Head away on a winding path that leads to a junction at the foot of Deep Dale **A**, where Deep Dale and Monyash are signed to the right. The path soon rejoins the stream crossed earlier, following it effortlessly into the valley.

Keep going along the shallowing dale to a gate. Slip through to continue on the other side, eventually emerging onto a broad track. Go left to a lane **B**. To the left it runs dead straight for almost ½ mile towards the Magpie workings, whose attendant buildings appear in distant view. Ignore the Sheldon turn-off, but leave at the bottom of the dip **C** for a path, which crosses the fields to the main pit head.

Today, the shell of a massive engine house and stout round chimney dominate the mine, which was worked for over 200 years until final closure in 1954. Flooding was an ever-present problem, temporarily solved with the introduction of early Cornish steam pumps. But they were unable to cope with the deepening workings and eventually, a mile (1.6km) long drainage sough was dug to the River Wye below Great Shacklow Wood.

Reconstructed horse gin

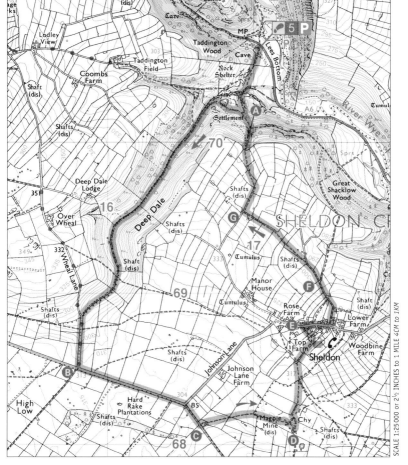

SCALE 1:25000 or 2½ INCHES to 1 MILE 4CM to 1KM

At a junction in front of the manager's cottage **D** go left (north), passing the circular ruin of the powder house, prudently distanced from all else in case of accident. Bear left to a stile in the corner and continue across an open field. Following a sign to Sheldon, carry on across a second field and then go right along a broad, walled track. Keep by the right wall beyond its end and in the next field swing left to a stile behind a corrugated barn. Cross to another stile by a small dew pond and walk through to emerge onto the main village street **E**.

Turn right past the **Cock and Pullet** but leave just beyond along a track on the left, signed to the church. Ignoring a junction, carry on for nearly ¼ mile, keeping an eye open for a stile on the left from which a path is signed to White Lodge and Deep Dale **F**. Head across to a second stile and stay by the wall, maintaining the same direction across subsequent fields. Eventually the way becomes contained past the hummocks of more mining activity to meet the end of a track **G**. Go right, and in the second field, slip across the wall to continue on its opposite flank. Towards the bottom, veer to a gate into the Deep Dale Nature Reserve. The ongoing path drops very steeply at the edge of Great Shacklow Wood. Meeting a lower path emerging from a wicket gate, walk left, the way falling more easily to the junction at Point **A**. Retrace your outward steps to the White Lodge car park. ●

Wormhill and Monk's Dale

		GPS waypoints
Start	Miller's Dale	🖊 SK 138 732
Distance	4¾ miles (7.6km)	Ⓐ SK 130 733
Height gain	920 feet (280m)	Ⓑ SK 127 734
Approximate time	2½ hours	Ⓒ SK 123 742
Parking	Car park at former station (Pay and Display)	Ⓓ SK 130 753
		Ⓔ SK 141 733
Route terrain	Field and uneven rocky paths through woodland	
Ordnance Survey maps	Landranger 119 (Buxton & Matlock), Explorer OL24 (The Peak District – White Peak area)	

From the Monsal Trail at the foot of Chee Dale, the walk climbs to the pretty hamlet of Wormhill, passing its attractive manor and small church. After following an old lane across the fields, the route returns through the delightful National Nature Reserve of Monk's Dale.

🖊 Follow the Monsal Trail from the old platforms of Miller's Dale Station west towards Chee Dale and Buxton. As you approach a viaduct spanning the Wye, the Monsal Trail is signed off right Ⓐ down a stepped path to the river below. Follow the riverbank upstream to a junction by a bridge at the foot of Chee Dale Ⓑ. Leaving the river, turn through a gate and follow an inclined path to Wormhill. Entering a meadow, curve right over the shoulder of the hill and climb along a narrow, wooded side-valley above a stream. Through a gate, continue past a cottage to emerge onto a lane. Head uphill past Wormhill Hall to the tiny village, there turning off along a side lane to the church Ⓒ.

Wormhill lay within the Royal Forest, where poaching was not the only threat to game and during the 14th century, a certain John Wolfhurt held land in return for hunting wolves out. The church, originally a chapel of ease to Tideswell, contains a memorial to James

Brindley, a local lad who established his reputation as an engineer in building the Bridgewater Canal.

Degrading to a track, the lane swings left. Leave just past a cottage along a short, contained path on the left. Keep ahead across successive narrow fields to meet a walled track and follow it right. It meanders between the fields for ½ mile to end in a sloping pasture. Accompany the onward hedge to a waymark and there bear left to a gate at the bottom onto a lane. Walk down to a stile in the dip on the right Ⓓ, and head across the pasture into the narrow confines of Monk's Dale.

Now dry, the upper gorge shelters a dense ash wood, whose dank, mossy understorey is rich in spring wildflowers. Lower down, the stream resurges and the valley opens to steep meadows on either side. Originally held by the Cluniac priory of Lenton, trouble arose during the 13th century after King John sought to sweeten the Bishop of

Coventry and Lichfield by gifting him the endowment. Lenton's protests were ignored until the monks took up arms and seized tithes stored in Tideswell church. Despite papal intervention, the dispute continued for three centuries until all became confiscated under Henry VIII's Dissolution.

Eventually breaking from the trees, the path continues across scrub meadow, rewarding a climb across the valley side with a superb view along the dale. Later passing back into woodland, the path drops to a bridge spanning the stream. Rising into the corner of a meadow, stay by the wall to a stile from which a twisting path descends to emerge beside the church **E**. Cross to the narrow lane opposite, signed to Litton Mill. Just past the site of an old corn mill and before reaching the **Angler's Rest**, turn off along a

Wormhill Hall and its grounds from the lane

waymarked path on the right, which crosses the mill leat and then the River Wye. Climb left to the embankment of the former railway and follow it right, back to Miller's Dale Station. ●

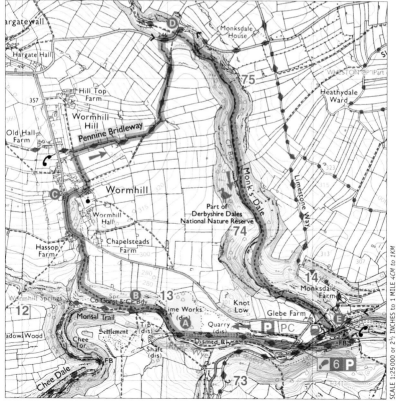

Longshaw and Padley Gorge

Start	Longshaw Country Park
Distance	5 miles (8km)
Height gain	840 feet (256m)
Approximate time	2½ hours
Parking	National Trust car park at start (Pay and Display)
Route terrain	Moorland tracks, woodland paths
Ordnance Survey maps	Landrangers 110 (Sheffield & Huddersfield) and 119 (Buxton & Matlock), Explorers OL24 (The Peak District – White Peak area) and OL1 (The Peak District – Dark Peak area)

GPS waypoints

- 🖉 SK 266 800
- Ⓐ SK 268 789
- Ⓑ SK 259 781
- Ⓒ SK 251 787
- Ⓓ SK 246 789
- Ⓔ SK 257 800

Open park, moor, dense woodland and a beautiful gorge lend great scenic variety to this walk. Add the historic interest of a 19th-century hunting lodge and a chapel wrought from a 14th-century manor and the result is a splendidly absorbing ramble.

🖉 From the bottom of the car park take the path down towards the visitor centre. After crossing a stream, turn left onto a track winding behind Longshaw Lodge signed to Wooden Pole Car Park. Now owned by the National Trust, Longshaw Country Park formed part of the Rutland estates, which were broken up in 1927. The palatial house was built a century earlier as a shooting lodge and after the sale was used as a guesthouse before being divided into private flats. Continue through the trees and then along a grass path, which runs at the foot of a low gritstone edge overlooking open parkland. Where it later splits, bear left, climbing to a road beside a junction.

Walk ahead, crossing the road from the right to a track leaving through a white-painted gate onto White Edge Moor Ⓐ. After passing the isolated White Edge Lodge, the way narrows to a grassy path that gradually loses height across the open moor. Bear left at a fork and continue down to meet the main road Ⓑ. Go left but almost at once cross and double back right through a gate returning into the Longshaw Estate. After ¼ mile, as the track meets a plantation of larch and pine, drop over a stile on the left and follow a gently descending path across bracken moorland. Approaching Oak's Wood, the way falls to the head of a wooded gorge. Ignore a crossing path and bear right on a path that loses height beside a lively stream cascading steeply through the trees. Approaching the bottom, keep left where the path splits, dropping to the road near a cottage Ⓒ.

A few yards to the left a path leaves sharp right, falling abruptly to Grindleford Station. Go right, crossing first the railway as it emerges from the 3½-mile (5.6km) Totley Tunnel and then bending over Burbage Brook by Padley Mill. Stay ahead past a junction, following the track a little farther to Padley Chapel, Ⓓ just beyond a row of houses.

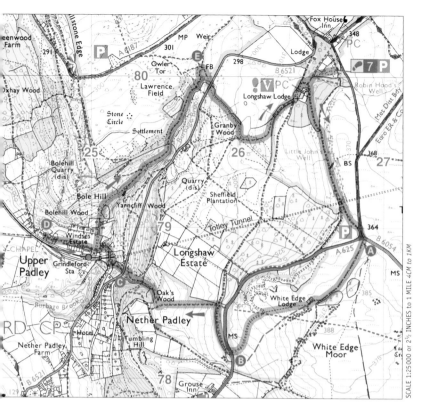

SCALE 1:25000 or 2½ INCHES to 1 MILE 4CM to 1KM

```
0    200   400   600   800 METRES  1
                                    KILOMETRES
                                    MILES
0    200   400   600 YARDS         ½
```

Sir Thomas Fitzherbert's 14th-century house fell into ruins and only the gate-house survives, which was converted into a chapel in 1933.

Return past the houses to the junction and go left, climbing to the top of the track where a gate takes the way into Padley Gorge, one of the few remnants of ancient woodland surviving in the Peak District. The gradient later eases and the onward path undulates above Burbage Brook, which tumbles cheerily over the rocks in a succession of miniature waterfalls. Emerging quite suddenly into open heath, there is a superb view ahead to the escarpment of Burbage Rocks. Carry on beside the stream to find a bridge **E**. Cross and climb right to the road above. Through a gate diagonally opposite, follow a path rising beside Granby Wood. After skirting a pond the way shortly breaks to more open ground, following a line of rhododendron bushes to a junction of paths in a clump of yew. Go through the left gate, passing below the front of the lodge to meet the main drive. Walk left, right and then left again back to the car park. ●

Padley Chapel

Chelmorton to Deep Dale

		GPS waypoints
Start	Wye Dale, 3 miles (4.8km) east of Buxton on the A6	🥾 SK 103 724
Distance	5¼ miles (8.4km)	Ⓐ SK 104 720
Height gain	810 feet (247m)	Ⓑ SK 096 707
Approximate time	2½ hours	Ⓒ SK 100 698
Parking	Car park beside A6 at start (Pay and Display)	Ⓓ SK 114 702
Route terrain	Rocky paths and field tracks	
Ordnance Survey maps	Landranger 119 (Buxton & Matlock), Explorer OL24 (The Peak District – White Peak area)	

A cursory glance at the map suggests an unprepossessing start to this ramble past the Topley quarries, but the workings are soon forgotten as you enter the Deep Dale Nature Reserve. Emerging along the tributary Horseshoe Dale, the route continues between the walled fields of the plateau to Chelmorton, where the pub might suggest a halfway halt. The leisurely return holds a final delight in the small but impressive gorge of Churn Hole.

🥾 From the Wye Dale car park, cross the road to a path signed beside the entrance to the Topley Pike Quarry. Passing a line of settling tanks, it

Thirst House Cave

quickly enters woodland, where the workings of the quarry are concealed behind high banks, and shortly reaches a wicket gate into the Deep Dale Nature Reserve Ⓐ.

The path immediately climbs steeply and gives a view into neighbouring Churn Hole before easing across the flank of the slope. Farther on the quarry is left behind and the way settles beside the intermittent stream flowing at the base of the confined dale. Acclivitous grassy slopes are rich in wild flowers such as bloody cranesbill and bell flower and even the seemingly sterile bands of sharp scree and rocky outcrops accommodate ferns and the occasional hazel. Higher up, the valley base harbours ash, the dank conditions encouraging swathes of moss upon the boulders. Look out too for Thirst House Cave, where excavations have revealed burials from the Stone Age, the bones of a brown bear and fragments of pottery from the Roman period. Local tales say it is the home of a hob or wood elf and claim that the spring issuing below will cure all ills of those bathing in it upon a Good Friday.

Eventually the restricted bounds of the gorge fall back and the path leaves the nature reserve over a stile. Carry on along a flat meadow at the top of which Horseshoe Dale branches left **B**. Shallower, but still littered with boulders it rises gently towards the plateau, finally passing the even

smaller, but private Bullhay Dale, where the cliff is pierced by a double-decker opening, the entrance to an old lead mine. Carry on to the head of Horseshoe Dale, leaving through a gate by a barn onto the main road.

Go left past Dale Grange Farm, taking to the fields just beyond over a stile on the left **C**. Accompany a broken wall away, bearing right in the next field to return to the road. Follow the verge left for 100 yds before turning right along a

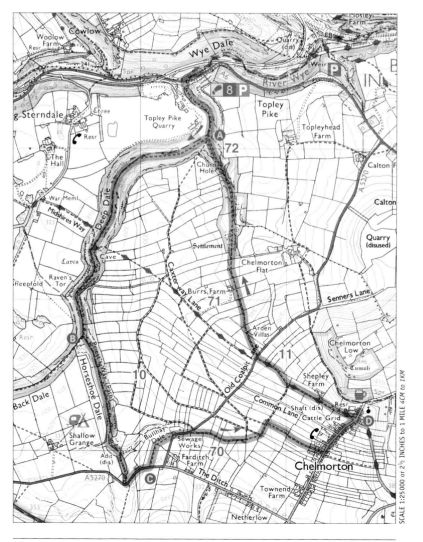

Deep Dale broadens out in its higher reaches

green, walled track. Entering a field, head for the far-left corner, crossing out onto another track. Go right and immediately left, looking for a wall stile some 70 yds along on the right. Walk the length of a couple of narrow fields, leaving beside a cottage to emerge on the main street in Chelmorton.

The heart of the village lies to the left, taking you past the Chelmorton Troughs. They are the sole survivors of several stone basins fed by a stream, delightfully named Illy Willy Water, which flowed through the village and provided water until the mains supply finally arrived after the Second World War. Carry on to the top of the lane where the two principal institutions of the community face each other, the **Church Inn** and church, the latter dating from at least the 13th century and having ancient grave markers and

coffin lids built into the walls of the Elizabethan porch.

Head a short distance back down the street before turning off right along a track **D** that leads to Shepley Farm. Bear left where it splits and continue between the fields to the main road. Cross to the track's continuation opposite. Through a gate at the end, keep going from field to field, bypassing Burrs Farm. Ignore a field track and stay ahead into the developing fold of a valley. Beyond a stile the way enters the gorge proper, concealed by trees and dropping steeply to Churn Hole over a rocky step, where those with short legs may need to use their hands. Small caves here yielded a Roman broach and animal bones when excavated at the end of the 19th century. Walk out down the valley to pick up your outward trail at the entrance to the Deep Dale Nature Reserve. ●

Pilsbury Castle

		GPS waypoints
Start	Hartington	
Distance	5½ miles (8.9km)	🖉 SK 128 604
Height gain	830 feet (253m)	Ⓐ SK 120 609
Approximate time	2½ hours	Ⓑ SK 115 624
Parking	In village	Ⓒ SK 115 632
Route terrain	Field paths and tracks	Ⓓ SK 115 638
Dog friendly	The bridge across the River Dove leaving Hartington has a metal grid base, which may be a problem for some dogs	Ⓔ SK 124 633 Ⓕ SK 130 612
Ordnance Survey maps	Landranger 119 (Buxton & Matlock), Explorer OL24 (The Peak District – White Peak area)	

In contrast to the confines of the lower dales, the hills enclosing upper Dovedale stand back as if to better appreciate the view. This ramble from the old market settlement of Hartington follows their example, contouring the high ground either side of the broad valley to visit the imposing site of an early Norman fortification.

🖉 From the centre of Hartington head in the direction of Pilsbury, turning left around the Corner House into Stonewell Lane. Approaching the former cheese factory, leave through a narrow gate on the right, where a field path is signed to Sheen. Beyond a strip of woodland, continue across another field to a stile in the far-left corner. Strike a diagonal to a second stile and maintain course to a footbridge spanning the River Dove. Over it, head for a gate in the top boundary beside a large tree to emerge onto a track Ⓐ.

Go right 150 yds to a stile on the left. A sign to Harris Close points an oblique line up a steep, gorse-covered bank. Over a stile at the top, walk within the fringe of a conifer plantation, breaking out to a superb prospect into the higher reaches of the valley. Carry on above the steep slope to a stile and, bearing left, follow a faint trod to another stile

at the field top. Accompany the ongoing wall to the farm at Harris Close, passing left of the buildings, through a yard, and out to a lane.

Walk right to find, after 200 yds, a path signed through a gate on the right Ⓑ. Take the stile immediately on the left, crossing a small rough paddock and then turn left along a short contained path to a stile behind a cottage. A slanting trod ushers you back towards the dale, making for the distant mounds of Pilsbury Castle seen on the opposite flank. Passing from the second field, the path briefly hugs a wall above the head of a marshy fold before resuming its downward trend. Meeting a walled track shaded by tall pine, head down to a footbridge and ford below Pilsbury Ⓒ.

Observant eyes will notice that the track's containing walls are of different materials, limestone on the left and sandstone to the right. The river here flows in the margin between the two types of rock, their diverse characters determining the vegetation and thus reflected in the general appearance of the opposing hillsides.

Over the river, the track climbs to a lane below Pilsbury Farm. Go left to a hairpin bend, and keep forward through a gate along another track. It continues up the valley to Pilsbury Castle, which is accessed through a gate at the end .

Despite the lack of stout curtain walls, high embattled towers and turreted keep, Pilsbury Castle presents a powerful image of formidable defence. It was built around the end of the 10th century by Henri de Ferrières, one of the French nobles who joined William's invasion of England in 1066. The earthen banks and ditches exploit the lie of the land and an outcrop of imposing limestone reef, their effectiveness originally heightened by wooden palisades along the top. Strategically overlooking the river, the fortification would have controlled the ford as well as passage up and down the valley and was probably built as a deterrent to further opposition following the failed northern rebellion. But as internal peace settled, it became redundant, being remote from the kingdom's borders.

After exploring the site, leave by the same gate and bear right on a rising path above the track along which you arrived. Reaching the crest, glance back to appreciate the castle's location and effectiveness as guardian of the valley and continue through a gap. The path levels above Pilsbury Farm, eventually swinging left across a final field to a narrow lane. Over a stile opposite, bear left to a wall gap and follow a trod along a broad, grassy fold, passing a gnarled marker stone to reach a distant wall.

Ignoring the stile, climb right to a small gate in the top corner. Head away, skirting a couple of corners before dropping to a gateway by a pair of tall trees. A distinct trod meanders across a

Above Bridge End Farm looking back to Beresford Dale

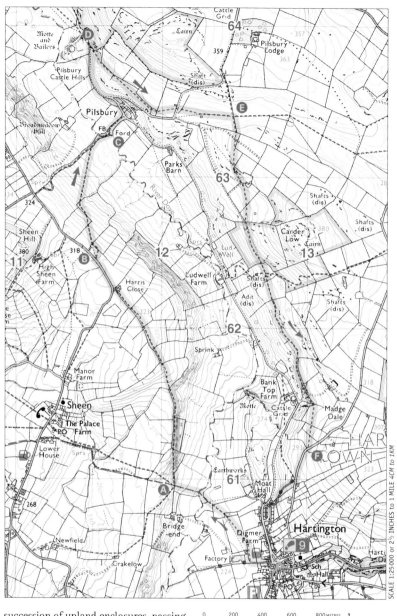

succession of upland enclosures, passing through an access area below Carder Low and then crossing a line of bell pit mines that followed a vein of lead ore across the hill. Eventually, the way runs above Bank Top Farm to meet the bend of a concrete track. Take the uphill branch, abandoning it as you pass into the higher field to stay with the right-hand wall to a stile. Continue across more fields, emerging over a final stile beyond a barn onto a lane **F**.

Walk down the hill, shortly turning off, just before a cream-painted cottage, onto a descending walled track. Coming out onto a lower lane, follow it left back into Hartington. ●

Chee Dale

		GPS waypoints
Start	Miller's Dale	
Distance	5¾ miles (9.3km)	SK 138 732
Height gain	1,290 feet (393m)	Ⓐ SK 130 733
Approximate time	3 hours	Ⓑ SK 127 734
Parking	Car park at former station (Pay and Display)	Ⓒ SK 112 726
Route terrain	Field and woodland paths, the one through Chee Dale being rocky, requiring occasional clambering and briefly along stepping stones that can be flooded during spate	Ⓓ SK 123 720
		Ⓔ SK 133 717
		Ⓕ SK 133 731
Ordnance Survey maps	Landranger 119 (Buxton & Matlock), Explorer OL24 (The Peak District – White Peak area)	

The River Wye's passage through the limestone gorges of the Peak is forever twisting, but nowhere is it more contorted than in the short, dramatic section above Miller's Dale known as Chee Dale. This secluded chasm is particularly beautiful and so constricted that, at one point, the river completely fills the narrow ravine and the path resorts to stepping stones. The walk returns across the upland fields and an old trackway ignored by the modern road network. The path through Chee Dale is occasionally flooded, but Walk 6 through Monk's Dale, also beginning along the Monsal Trail, offers an alternative ramble for the day.

Leaving the car park, walk past the old platforms of Miller's Dale Station and follow the track right, signed as the Monsal Trail to Chee Dale and Buxton. Beyond the East Buxton Lime Kilns, a high viaduct carries the former railway across the River Wye to the portal of a tunnel burrowing beneath Chee Tor, but through which there is now no passage. Instead, leave the trail immediately after the viaduct. Go through a couple of gates on the right Ⓐ and follow a descending trod, again signed to Chee Dale, across a hillside meadow to a footbridge over the river.

On the opposite bank Ⓑ, scale a stile on the left and head upriver until the path veers above the gushing eruptions of Wormhill Springs. After crossing a footbridge at the foot of Flag Dale, the path resumes its course up Chee Dale, clambering over rocks and then passing beneath towering, overhung cliffs dripping water. Higher up, the gorge narrows further and the path is forced into the riverbed along a string of sturdy stepping stones. *Should the river be in spate and the stepping stones impassable, you can rescue the day by going back to Point Ⓑ and following*

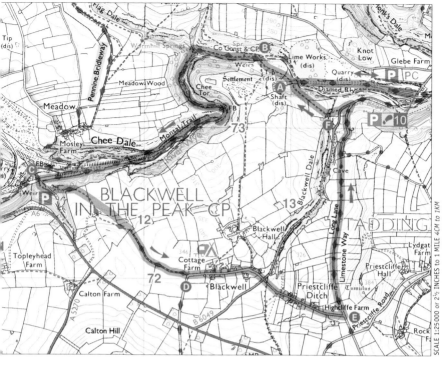

SCALE 1:25000 or 2½ INCHES to 1 MILE 4CM to 1KM

Walk 6 through Wormhill and Monk's Dale instead.

Returning to dry ground around the bend, go over a footbridge below a lofty viaduct and carry on at a higher level above the river. After a short distance, double back at a Monsal Trail sign to Blackwell Mill, climbing to the disused railway as it emerges from beneath Chee Tor. Walk across the viaduct and through a short tunnel to continue high above the river. Despite the elevation and superb prospect into the gorge, the position remains dwarfed by the soaring cliffs containing the deep rift.

Over 300 feet (91m) deep and, at one point, completely taken up by the river, Chee Dale is one of the most spectacular sections of the River Wye's valley. Bound by high, overhanging limestone cliffs, it presented a considerable challenge to the engineers of the

London Midland Railway as they forced their line towards Manchester. The railway from Derby reached Buxton in 1863 and was continued north via Great Rocks Dale when the Dove Holes Tunnel opened a couple of years later. As well

The stepping stones in Chee Dale

The railway enters the narrow gorge of Chee Dale

as carrying considerable passenger traffic, the line enabled vast quarries to be developed within the gorge. The stone was burnt in massive kilns built beside the track to produce quicklime, a substance demanded in huge quantities by the building, chemical and smelting industries as well as for use as an agricultural fertiliser. The East Buxton Lime Kilns, which you earlier passed, opened in 1880 and were in operation until 1944.

Beyond another short tunnel the trail again swaps banks and soon forks at a junction that took the line through Great Rocks Dale via Chinley to Manchester. However, stick with the left branch along Wye Dale, which led to Buxton, in a little while passing beneath a bridge ❻. Over a stile on the left, climb to the track above and follow it from the bridge up a narrow side valley.

Part-way up, a path is signed to Blackwell over a stile on the left. Zigzagging steeply, it pauses at a promontory overlooking Wye Dale, from which there is a magnificent view. Leaving the prospect, continue up the hill to then level beside a wall. Over a

stile keep going in the adjacent field, but in the next field, veer to a gate in the distant corner. Stay by the right wall to a second gate, joining a track up to meet the Pennine Bridleway. Follow it left through a gate and on across the fields to meet the corner of a lane ❼.

Walk ahead past the scattered dwellings of Blackwell, continuing over a crossroads towards Priestcliffe and Taddington. Where the rising lane eventually bends sharp right, abandon it for a broad, walled track on the left, the Limestone Way ❽. Aptly named Long Lane, the track steadily loses height for the next $^3/_4$ mile, revealing a superb view into Wye Dale and the foot of Monk's Dale. It eventually leads to the B6049, just west of Miller's Dale.

Go left to the bend, leaving there over a stile on the right ❾. Drop left, across a sloping meadow to a stream emanating from Blackwell Dale and cross to a stile on the opposite bank. Climb steeply to the top-right corner of the meadow. Pass through the broken corner of the bounding wall and follow a path falling between the trees into the valley. It ends over a stile onto the Monsal Trail at Point ❿. Go back over the viaduct to the Miller's Dale car park. ●

Ashford in the Water and Monsal Dale

		GPS waypoints	
Start	Ashford in the Water		
Distance	6 miles (9.7km)	🖊	SK 194 697
Height gain	1,130 feet (344m)	Ⓐ	SK 191 701
		Ⓑ	SK 184 715
Approximate time	3 hours	Ⓒ	SK 181 717
Parking	Car park in village	Ⓓ	SK 170 706
Route terrain	Clear tracks and woodland paths	Ⓔ	SK 189 694
Ordnance Survey maps	Landranger 119 (Buxton & Matlock), Explorer OL24 (The Peak District – White Peak area)		

This superb woodland and riverside walk through Monsal Dale links an idyllic village to one of the finest viewpoints in the Peak District. Of interest is an imposing viaduct condemned by Ruskin and the ruins of an old mill as well as several features in the village itself.

Ashford in the Water is an attractive village of 18th- and 19th-century cottages, built of rugged limestone clustered around a church. The 'water' of its name is the River Wye, and the village grew up at a safe crossing point – a ford by ash trees. In the 17th century the three-arched packhorse bridge, known as the Sheepwash Bridge, was constructed. It is so called because

Ashford in the Water

Pennyunk Lane

sheep were washed in the river here at shearing time. Although of Norman foundation, the church was largely rebuilt in the late 19th century. Inside there is a table of black Ashford 'marble', made from the local common grey limestone, which when polished becomes black and shiny, resembling expensive marble.

🖊 Out of the car park behind the church, walk forward along Court Lane to a junction and turn right into Vicarage Lane. After 50 yds double back left on a footpath signed to Monsal Dale, turning up to climb beside houses and enter a field at the top. Guided by a waymark, strike across to find a stile in the far right corner, emerging onto a walled track, Pennyunk Lane Ⓐ.

Follow it left for ¾ mile, enjoying a splendid vista across the neatly walled rolling countryside. Through a squeeze stile at its end, walk away by a wall on your left. Immediately through a gate at the next corner turn right past a dewpond. Joining the end of another track keep going forward, soon emerging at a viewpoint above Monsal Dale. Swing right along the lip of the valley, the path losing height across the steep slope to meet a lane at Monsal Head Ⓑ.

This vantage point, overlooking a right-angled turn of the river, is probably the finest along the valley. The Wye, far below at the bottom of steep-sided, wooded slopes, winds serenely, the whole crossed by a railway viaduct standing prominently in the scene. Victorian conservationists, led by Ruskin, decried it as an ugly intrusive structure, bitterly opposing its construction in 1863 as a desecration of the dale. However, time has weathered the viaduct to harmonise with its surroundings and it has now become one with the landscape. The viaduct carried the Midland Railway route from St Pancras to Manchester, which here ran between Bakewell and Buxton. The railway closed in 1968, but the bridge continues in service as part of the Monsal Trail, a footpath following the course of the Wye from outside Buxton all the way to Bakewell.

Instead of joining the lane, take the descending path signed as access to the viaduct, but at a junction part-way down, keep ahead into Monsal Dale. Reaching the bottom of the valley, turn left through a gate immediately after a cottage and barn to a footbridge across the river Ⓒ.

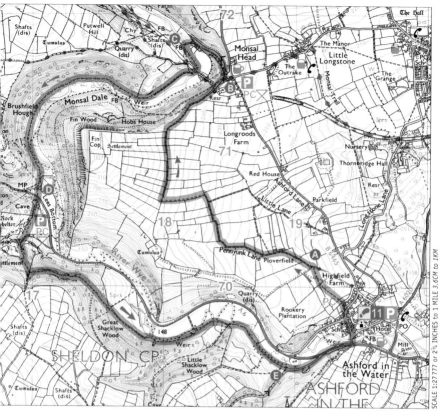

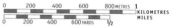

Follow the Wye downstream, passing beneath the viaduct to enjoy a delightful walk of some 1¼ miles. As the valley narrows, the path meanders on through a jumble of native woodland. Beyond a weir, the river too takes on a more natural character, swirling in deep pools. Reaching a fork at the edge of the wood, bear left towards White Lodge and the A6.

Emerging onto the main road **D**, make for the car park opposite. The onward path leaves beside the payment machine, rising through the picnic area to a gate. Keep going over another meadow towards the mouth of Deep Dale, ignoring an intermediate path to Taddington. Joining a stream, briefly follow it up and then cross to a wall stile. Walk directly from the stile on a rising path winding through craggy, open woodland to a junction. Turn left

to Ashford and Sheldon, still climbing to another junction in front of a gate. The route to Ashford lies ahead, now undulating more easily through Great Shacklow Wood. Ignore a crossing path and descend at the edge of the wood to join the river, the way shortly passing the ruin of an old watermill, employed for crushing bones to make fertiliser.

Disregarding the track out to the A6, continue ahead over a stile beside a gate across a succession of meadows, eventually meeting a lane **E**. Go left to the main road and follow that right for some 300 yds to Sheepwash Bridge. Cross the river back into Ashford and walk ahead along Fennel Street, where you will find the car park on the right, a short way along. ●

Tissington and Alsop en le Dale

Start	Tissington
Distance	6¼ miles (10.1km)
Height gain	820 feet (250m)
Approximate time	3 hours
Parking	Pay and Display at eastern end of village by Tissington Trail
Route terrain	Field paths and tracks
Ordnance Survey maps	Landranger 119 (Buxton & Matlock), Explorer OL24 (The Peak District – White Peak area)

GPS waypoints

🖉	SK 178 520
Ⓐ	SK 172 526
Ⓑ	SK 164 537
Ⓒ	SK 155 549
Ⓓ	SK 161 551
Ⓔ	SK 182 545
Ⓕ	SK 175 535

This corner of the Peak District abounds in idyllic, unspoiled and uncommercialised villages of warm, honey-coloured limestone, two of the finest being visited in this pleasant ramble. Also featured are two short stretches of the Tissington Trail, a former railway line now usefully converted to a bridleway and giving glorious sweeping views over the surrounding countryside.

Blessed with an avenue of limes where cottages are set back behind wide verges, a church, manorial hall and a pretty pond, Tissington has an air of timeless serenity and seems the quintessential English village. Part of the effect is undoubtedly due to the fact that Tissington is very much an estate village and has been continuously in the possession of one family, the Fitzherberts, since the 15th century. The family still lives in the fine early 17th-century hall, which has been extended and rebuilt several times over the centuries. The simple church, over-looking both hall and village from its mound, retains much Norman work despite a thorough restoration in Victorian times. It possesses a number of monuments to the Fitzherberts, as well as a rare Saxon font. Many of Tissington's cottages date from a

rebuilding programme carried out between 1830 and 1860 that included the village school, now a tearoom, built in the year of Queen Victoria's accession (1837).

Although many villages in Derbyshire now hold annual well-dressing ceremonies, none is more associated with this ancient tradition than Tissington. The several wells are decorated with tableaux, which usually depict biblical themes and are made from pressing flowers, ferns, mosses, leaves and bark onto wooden frames covered with clay. The results are strikingly beautiful and ornate. The origins of this custom are somewhat obscure, but the conventional theory is that it started in the middle of the 14th century during the Black Death as a thanksgiving by the villagers for escaping the plague through the purity of the waters. It has not been a continuous custom and may have been first revived in Tissington as a result of the wells not running dry during a great drought in 1615. Whatever the ceremony's origin, well dressing is a colourful spectacle that attracts many visitors to Tissington on Ascension Day and on various dates throughout the summer months to the other villages in the area, which have taken up the custom.

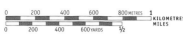 From the car park on the site of the former station, walk up to the lane and keep left to a small green at the village centre. Go right below the church to climb past Tissington Hall. Keep ahead along Rakes Lane until it bends sharply left beyond the village **A**. Quit it there, not along the track in front, but over a stile beside a gate to its left. Strike across the slope, continuing from field to field and shortly passing above Broadclose Farm. Keep going,

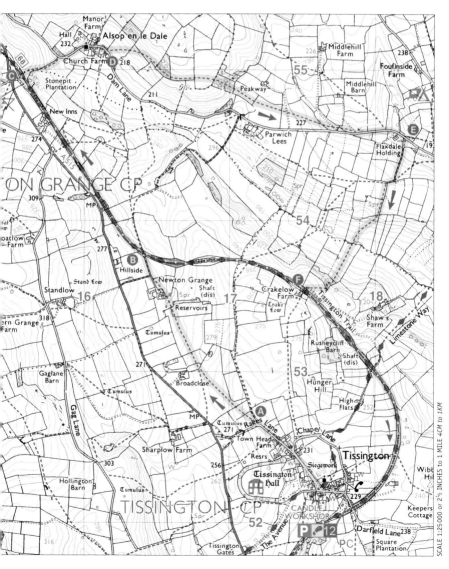

negotiating more stiles towards the next farm, Newton Grange. After dropping through a dip, skirt the farm buildings to the right and then curve left to escape from the top corner of the field onto a track. Turn right and subsequently keep ahead to a bridge. Leave just before it through a gate on the right, climbing up to join the Tissington Trail **B**.

This was part of the railway line from Ashbourne to Buxton, which opened in 1899 but finally closed in 1967. Fortunately, the Peak Planning Board swiftly purchased large sections of it (and also other lines that closed around the same time) and created a superb bridleway that runs for 13 miles (21km) between Parsley Hay and Ashbourne, readily accessible by all.

Follow the trail left for a mile to reach a car park. Just past it **C**, look for a stile on the right. Following a sign to Alsop en le Dale, head downhill, crossing the accompanying wall through a gap about halfway along to continue on its opposite flank. Emerging at the bottom over a stile onto a lane, turn right into the village. Although smaller and less frequented than Tissington, it has a similar picturesque combination of attractive Norman church and old hall surrounded by houses, cottages and farms.

Walk through the village to find a stile just past the last house on the left **D**. Climb diagonally across a couple of fields to a stile in the top wall, turning right above it to another stile entering a small coppice wood. At the far side, keep going by a wall and then over further stiles, soon descending through more trees and along the succeeding fields. Eventually meeting a track, cross and make for the bottom right-hand corner of the next field. Through the hedge, go over a second track to find a small gate beneath a holly tree diagonally opposite. Continue at the bottom edge of this final field before leaving through a gate onto a lane. Follow it to the left for a little less than ¼ mile.

Just past a complex of barns, look for a waymarked stile on the right **E**. Entering a field, head for a narrow gate in the right corner, from which an old, hedged track rises. Through another gate at the top swing right to negotiate a stile, there following the field edge to the left. In the next field, keep going over the hill and then, after crossing the sparse hedge of an old boundary, bear right across the falling slope. Over a bridged ditch resume a direct descent to a bridge spanning the stream that courses the valley bottom. Climb straight up the opposite hill, eventually reaching a gate in the top wall. With the worst of the ascent now behind you, bear half-right to a stile beside a gate **F**.

In front is a railway bridge, but instead of crossing, go over another stile on the left, from which a path slopes to the Tissington Trail. To the left, it leads back to the car park from which the walk began, offering some fine views along the way. ●

One of Tissington's several wells

Beeley and Hob Hurst's House

Beeley and Hob Hurst's House

Start	Beeley	GPS waypoints	
Distance	6¼ miles (10.1km)		SK 265 674
Height gain	950 feet (290m)	Ⓐ	SK 265 676
		Ⓑ	SK 270 684
Approximate time	3 hours	Ⓒ	SK 271 690
Parking	Considerate roadside parking in the village	Ⓓ	SK 278 685
		Ⓔ	SK 287 692
Route terrain	Good tracks and clear field paths	Ⓕ	SK 282 687
		Ⓖ	SK 279 675
Ordnance Survey maps	Landranger 119 (Buxton & Matlock), Explorer OL24 (The Peak District – White Peak area)	Ⓗ	SK 269 666

The high moors were not always as deserted as they appear today, once supporting communities of farmers who have left their mark in traces of field systems and innumerable burial mounds. One of the most unusual is known as Hob Hurst's House and is visited on this walk from the pretty estate village of Beeley. The route contrasts open hillside with thick woodland plantation and offers outstanding views across the Derwent Valley.

Although close to Chatsworth, Beeley retained its independence until the third Duke began acquiring the neighbouring

Climbing onto Beeley Moor

land to extend his estate. Over time, cottages, a reading room, school and new chapel were put up for the benefit of the estate workers and the Norman church dedicated to St Anne was largely

rebuilt, although vestiges of the original work survive around the doorway and in carved heads gazing down from the walls. The **village inn**, which has earned a reputation for its food, dates from the 17th century, when in addition to farming, coal mining and stone quarrying were important industries, while just south of the village the stream cascading down the hillside powered a lead smelting mill.

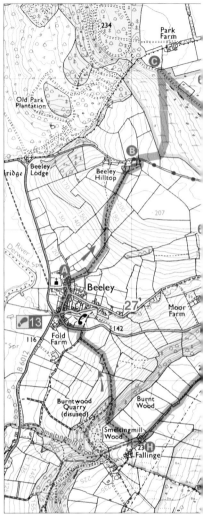

✎ Take the street opposite the **Devonshire Arms**, climbing through the village beside the **Old Smithy café**. Keep left at a triangular green, passing the entrance to the church car park. Just beyond, look for a squeeze stile set back on the right behind New House **Ⓐ**. Head away, along a narrow pasture, continuing in a second field to the distant top-left corner. A slanting trod carries on to the brow of the hill, over which the way follows a wall to Beeley Hilltop. Walk past the farmhouse and keep right in front of cow sheds before turning left through a yard to emerge onto a track **Ⓑ**.

A few yards to the right, go over a stile on the left. Bear right to a second stile onto the open moor. A clear path left strikes an oblique ascent across a steep, bracken-clad hillside, broaching the top to meet a broad track **Ⓒ**.

Take time to admire the view back across the valley before following the track gently uphill to the right. Approaching the crest, look for a waymarked path leaving on the left **Ⓓ**. Strike across the tussock moor towards the corner of Bunker's Hill Wood. Through a gate there, carry on beside the bounding wall, climbing past the end of Harland Edge to a crossing track at the top corner of the plantation. The prehistoric burial site of Hob Hurst's House then lies only a short distance to the right **Ⓔ**.

The early Bronze Age burial mound was first excavated by the Victorian antiquarian Thomas Bateman. Born at nearby Rowsley, he followed his father's interest in archaeology and investigated so many ancient burials that he became known as the 'Barrow Knight'. He opened Hob Hurst's House in 1853 to find fragments of burnt human bones and pieces of lead ore. Unusually, the burial is angular rather than round and the inner chamber, walled with upright slabs, is surrounded by a ditch and earth bank. The beliefs of these ancient peoples have been lost in time, but such monuments demonstrate a reverence for ancestors

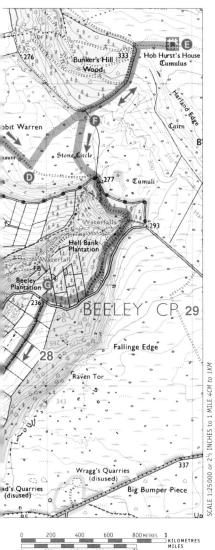

left appeasing offerings of milk, ale or even a suit of clothes.

Some 300 yds east of the burial is an ancient stone cross or waymark, interesting for the quaint three-fingered hands showing 'Bakewell Road', 'Chesterfeild Road' and 'Sheaffeild Roade'. Unfortunately there is none pointing south, the direction you want, so you must retrace your steps past Hob Hurst's House and follow the wall back down the hill beside the plantation.

Just after passing through the gate and crossing a planked ditch, watch for a fork in the path . Branch left and keep left where it again splits to meet the end of a track (the one you left earlier) at the corner of Hell Bank Plantation. Over a stile beside a gate, cross to another gate opposite, from which a path leads into the trees. At a fork, go left, shortly crossing a stream and reaching a second fork. Now bear right, descending across the wooded slope of the valley. Carry on as a path joins and then, where the way divides, choose the right branch, before long meeting a lane. However, remain in the wood along a path beside the wall, which ultimately leads to a stile .

Cross to the gated track opposite, a bridleway that runs pleasantly between walled fields below Fallinge Edge for ³/₄ mile. Approaching Fallinge Farm and immediately after a large barn, turn off right along a grass bridleway signed to Rowsley. After only 70 yds, leave over a stile on the right and strike across the field to another stile. A path drops sharply left and then almost immediately right across the steep bank of Smeltingmill Wood. Emerging from the trees, maintain the diagonal across a couple of meadows and then turn down beside the boundary. Reaching the bottom, go right at the foot of a final field onto the lane. Beeley is then just a short walk to the left. ●

SCALE 1:25000 or 2½ INCHES to 1 MILE 4CM to 1KM

0   200   400   600   800 METRES   1
                              KILOMETRES
0   200   400   600 YARDS   ½   MILES

and affirm a belonging to the land.

Hob Hurst is a Derbyshire goblin about whom tales are widespread throughout the Peak. He frequented caves, wooded hollows, stone circles and burial mounds and there are many 'houses' where he supposedly lived. It paid to stay in his good books, for he might then clean the house or ensure the milking went well, but cross him and ill luck was likely to follow. Some folk kept clear of his lairs while others

Brand Side and the Source of the Dove

		GPS waypoints
Start	Hollinsclough	SK 065 664
Distance	6½ miles (10.5km)	Ⓐ SK 063 668
Height gain	1,230 feet (375m)	Ⓑ SK 058 681
Approximate time	3 hours	Ⓒ SK 047 693
Parking	Roadside parking	Ⓓ SK 037 694
Route terrain	Rough field and moorland paths	Ⓔ SK 038 683
Ordnance Survey maps	Landranger 119 (Buxton & Matlock), Explorer OL24 (The Peak District – White Peak area)	Ⓕ SK 044 676
		Ⓖ SK 048 672

The River Dove gathers its waters from the bleak, peaty slopes of Axe Edge Moor, falling rapidly through deep gritstone cloughs towards the limestone country of the south east. The scenery here could hardly be a greater contrast to that found in the gorges of its middle reaches and reflects the origins of the river's name, dubo meaning 'dark' or 'black'. Beginning from the tiny hamlet of Hollinsclough, the walk encircles the head valley, crossing Cistern's Clough, the highest source stream and returning past Dove Head.

This is frontier country, where grit and limestone meet; a rugged terrain that, despite the patchwork of enclosures shown on the map, has hardly been tamed. The tussock and heather of the moors above spill onto rough pastures of poor grazing, often made marshy by oozing springs welling from below the course turf. To the east and south, the limestone dramatically breaks out in a series of sharp ridges which, from a distance, appear as giant waves in a frozen sea. But, despite its apparent abandonment, this was a well-travelled route in and out of the Peak, evidenced by several ancient packhorse bridges.

🖉 Take the lane west out of Hollinsclough towards Flash. After 200 yds leave through a signed gate on the right. Where it shortly forks, keep right and head into the lower pasture, where a stone bridge spans the infant River Dove Ⓐ. Through a gate above, bear

Packhorse bridge across the River Dove

| 0 | 200 | 400 | 600 | 800 METRES | 1 |
| 0 | 200 | 400 | 600 YARDS | ½ | KILOMETRES / MILES |

left on a rising path to join a rough track and continue along the valley side. Keep going past a lonely cottage, Fough, eventually emerging over a cattle-grid onto the end of a lane near Booth Farm.

Follow it for 50 yds before leaving over a stile on the left opposite a small pond **B**. Strike left to a stile in the side wall and maintain the line behind the farm to a third stile. Head away along the rough pastures of the valley on a developing trod that later crosses the

stream at its base. Move above the stream to join a field track that rises to another farm, Thirkelow. Pass through the yard and continue out to a lane.

Go left, but then leave after 100 yds along another farm track on the left **C**. Keep ahead as it then forks, walking down to Fairthorn Farm. Entering the yard, turn right past the front of the cottage. Climb away above the deep and narrow Cistern's Clough, which is the highest tributary of the River Dove. Reaching a stone packhorse bridge, cross and walk up to a lane.

Turn right up the hill to find, after 200 yds a stile on the left **D**. Cross a rough enclosure and stay beside the wall up to a gate. Bear left to the far corner of the next enclosure and, crossing a couple of stiles, follow a grassy gully downhill to a gate and stile behind a farm. Walk through the garden yard, turning right in front of the farmhouse to leave through a gap in the wall. Negotiate a marshy area surrounding a spring and head away across the slope of the hill, picking up the line of a broken wall to the next farm. Pass through its yard and leave along the drive. Through the gate at the bottom of a dip, cross a stile on the right. Pick up a developing trod that leads across successive fields to another farm. Drop out behind the farmhouse and follow its track to meet a narrow lane at Dove Head.

Walk downhill to a bridge, just beyond which is a stile on the left **E**. Head away past a redundant stile, sticking with a line of old fence posts above the rapidly deepening valley of the River Dove. Carry on from field to field until you reach a stile on the right, by a power cable post below Nether Colshaw Farm. Over it, strike a left diagonal upfield, maintaining the

Chrome Hill is a spectacular landmark

slanting line across subsequent enclosures to emerge onto the end of a track **F**. Cross to a stone stile beside the metal field gate opposite and head downhill beside the left wall. Towards the bottom, the wall kinks back to a gated squeeze stile. Follow a narrow walled track down to the right, coming out beside the entrance to Lower Colshaw Barn. Continue ahead on a rough lane.

Reaching a junction **G**, go left, but after a few yards, bear off right onto an old packhorse trail. Eventually joining a stream, it winds into the valley, where a graceful stone bridge spans the Dove. Ignore the bridge and instead cross the side stream to a stile from which a path is signed to Hollinsclough. The river rapidly falls below the path, which settles for a higher line across the steep sided valley cloaked in scrub gorse and stunted trees. Keep left where the path forks by a clump of holly, the slope beyond opening to rough pasture. Walk on, going past a barn, crossing a broken wall and then later in more trees, a stile. Eventually, the bridge crossed at the beginning of the walk appears far below. Stay ahead, to rejoin your outward track back to Hollinsclough. ●

The Goyt Valley and Shining Tor

Start	Errwood Reservoir	**GPS waypoints**	
Distance	6½ miles (10.5km)	🖊	SK 012 748
Height gain	1,310 feet (399m)	Ⓐ	SK 001 761
		Ⓑ	SJ 995 767
Approximate time	3½ hours	Ⓒ	SJ 994 737
Parking	Car park at start. On bank	Ⓓ	SK 000 729
	holidays and summer Sundays	Ⓔ	SK 011 730
	park at Pym Chair and begin from	Ⓕ	SK 011 735
	Ⓑ because of road closures		
Route terrain	Generally clear moorland paths		
Ordnance Survey maps	Landrangers 118 (Stoke-on-Trent & Macclesfield) and 119 (Buxton & Matlock), Explorer OL24 (The Peak District – White Peak area)		

The character of the Goyt Valley has altered over the last half-century. The vale's former isolation has ebbed before an influx of car-borne visitors and its natural lines changed by the construction of reservoirs and planting of conifers. Despite these intrusions upon the moorland, woods and streams, it remains a valley of outstanding beauty, the lakes and forests another facet of diversity. This walk encompasses its most interesting features and grandest scenery, climbing past the scanty ruins of an abandoned hall and unusual shrine. An airy ridge walk to the summit of Shining Tor reveals splendid views on both sides before the way drops back into the wooded valley.

The Goyt Valley was formerly a remote area of wild and open country lying between two royal hunting grounds, Peak Forest to the east and Macclesfield Forest to the west. It was partially 'tamed' in the 19th century, both by the activities of the Grimshawe family, who built Errwood Hall and laid out the surrounding ornamental gardens and by the growth of industry in the area, notably quarrying and coal-mining. More major and significant changes to its landscape took place during the last century with the damming of the river by Stockport Corporation to create two reservoirs, Fernilee in 1938 and Errwood in 1967 and, from 1963, the Forestry Commission's planting of large blocks of conifers, mainly on the western slopes.

🖊 Leave the rear of the car park by an information board, climbing the grassy slope to a gap in the upper wall. Go right on a track that shortly curves left through a steep and narrow wooded valley. Part-way up, turn sharp right, soon passing below the ruins of Errwood Hall. It was built in 1830 by

Looking back from Oldgate Nick

the Grimshawes, a Roman Catholic family who owned much of the valley and contemporary photographs show a handsome and palatial, Italian-looking residence surrounded by exotic landscaped gardens. However, the hall was abandoned and demolished in the 1930s as the waters of the first of the reservoirs started to rise. Today, the meagre ruins retain an attractively melancholic air, but rhododendrons and azaleas, vestiges of the ornamental gardens, still bloom resplendent during late May and June.

The path continues above a stream, shortly dipping to cross. On the far bank, turn right and then left at successive junctions to climb below Foxlow Edge, the way signed towards the Shrine and Pym Chair. There is an excellent view of the ridge soon to be traversed before you reach the Spanish Shrine, a simple, circular building of local gritstone but undeniably Mediterranean in inspiration and design. It was erected by the Grimshawes in 1889 in memory of a much-loved Spanish governess in their employ.

Beyond the shrine the path rises

steadily and it is then not far to the lane **Ⓐ**. Turn up the hill but leave as you approach the brow through a gate in the wall on the left **Ⓑ**.

The viewpoint, known as Pym Chair, commands a superb panorama over the Goyt woodlands and surrounding hills. It lies at the crossing of ancient routes, one of which was a 'saltway' from the Cheshire salt-producing district around Northwich and Nantwich that ran across the Pennines to Chesterfield and Sheffield.

Through the gate, a path signed to Shining Tor climbs and settles along the ridge beside a stone wall. It offers a grand walk for over 1¼ miles (2.8km), rising first over Cats Tor (1,703 feet/519m) and then onto Shining Tor (1,833 feet/559m), where a triangulation pillar marking the summit lies over a ladder-stile to the right **Ⓒ**. There is a splendid view in all directions across the rolling hills and bare moorlands, the distinctive conical shape of Shutlingsloe clearly visible, some three miles (4.8km) to the south.

Returning to the path, follow it down across a saddle to a kissing-gate, through which is a crossing path. Turn right, shortly passing through a gate to find, immediately beyond, a stile on the left **Ⓓ**. Signed to Goyt's Clough Quarry, a path drops beside a wall. Reaching the corner of a forest, which is being progressively harvested and replanted, the way skirts its perimeter, in time crossing a track into the plantation. Ignore it and keep going outside the fence until eventually, you reach a stile. Cross and follow a winding path down to a bridge spanning a stream. Climb left to a fork above the far bank **Ⓔ** and keep left on a permissive path that tacks above the brook falling through Deep Clough, coming out at the bottom onto a narrow lane by the abandoned quarries. You can then simply follow the lane left back to the car park, but a more interesting path can be found a short way along as you enter a stand of trees **F**. Signed off right as the Riverside

Walk, it drops to follow the Goyt downstream, returning later to the lane. Cross diagonally to the gated continuation of the track, now signed to Errwood Hall. It rises above the lane and later, the car park, which is then signed off as you approach. ●

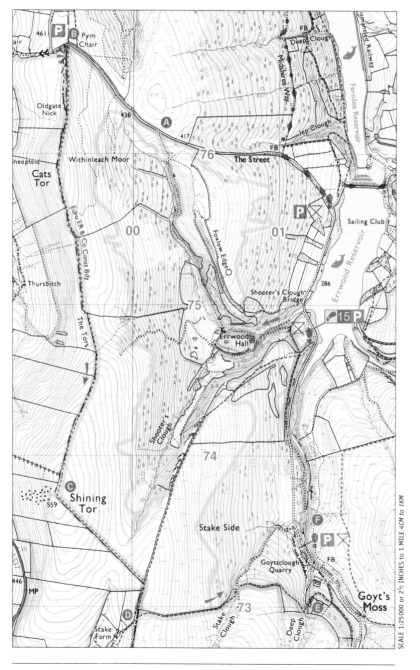

The Manifold Valley

		GPS waypoints
Start	Wetton	🔖 SK 109 551
Distance	6½ miles (10.5km)	Ⓐ SK 109 554
Height gain	1,420 feet (433m)	Ⓑ SK 104 572
Approximate time	3½ hours	Ⓒ SK 095 584
Parking	Car park at edge of village	Ⓓ SK 091 577
Route terrain	Field paths and valley trails, steep descent to Ecton	Ⓔ SK 098 550
Ordnance Survey maps	Landranger 119 (Buxton & Matlock), Explorer OL24 (The Peak District – White Peak area)	

The Manifold flows roughly parallel with the Dove through similarly attractive limestone scenery, but its valley is generally quieter and less well known. The name Manifold means literally many folds or turns and is an apt one, for the river forms a whole series of loops and meanders along its length. From the village of Wetton the route takes an undulating course across the fields, passing the remains of abandoned copper mines and eventually climbing to a most dramatic and expansive viewpoint overlooking the Manifold Valley. After a steep descent into the dale there is a lovely walk along the Manifold Track, a disused railway line that keeps by the winding river. The return to Wetton passes the impressive Thor's Cave, without doubt the dominant feature of the surrounding landscape.

The small, remote and seemingly unchanging village of Wetton lies on the eastern slopes of the Manifold Valley, its attractive grey stone cottages grouped around a pub and medieval church, a short and plain building with a rather heavy-looking tower.

🔖 From the car park turn left along a lane and left again at a road junction, walking through the village to pass the **Royal Oak Inn** and then the church. Where the road bends left, bear off along a track, which is subsequently signed to Back of Ecton Ⓐ. Through a gateway at the top, walk ahead negotiating a couple of gap stiles to

gain the National Trust land of Wetton Hill. A grassy trod guides you from field to field, soon meeting and following a wall below the flanks of Wetton Hill as a grand view opens ahead.

Remain with the wall until it turns, there keeping ahead towards the far bottom field corner. Walk forward across the marshy gatherings of a stream to a stile, climbing to a gate, just left of the top-right corner of the field beyond. Go right to meet a lane Ⓑ. Turn left, zigzagging up the hill to leave just before the brow through a gate on the right. Head diagonally up, joining a wall that guides you to the abandoned

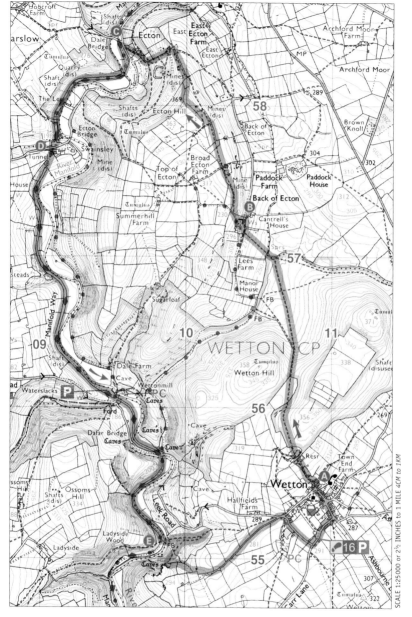

ruins of a copper mine. The ore deposits were some of the richest in Europe and the shafts and levels honeycombing the hill made a fortune for the fifth Duke of Devonshire. Carry on over a stile, initially beside a wall and then breaking from it to make a beeline past the spoil tips of more workings for a triangulation pillar on the summit of Ecton Hill. From it,

the ground falls dramatically into the Manifold Valley with the village of Warslow topping the opposite hill. Beneath your feet are Dale Bridge and a curious house, more reminiscent of the Rhineland than Staffordshire.

The Manifold Valley

magnificent valley came by its name.

After a little over $^1/_2$ mile, the way joins a lane **D**. Keep going through a tunnel, following the lane beyond for a further mile to a junction opposite Wetton Mill. The mill, accessed over an old packhorse bridge, ground corn until it closed in 1857 but now restored by the National Trust, continues as a **tearoom** and holiday cottages.

Resume the riverside trail below sheer limestone cliffs, shortly crossing the river. At a junction, keep ahead over another bridge, beyond which Thor's Cave soon comes into view, a gaping hole high in the cliff overlooking the narrow gorge. Approaching its foot, abandon the track **E** for a footbridge across the river.

On the other side, the path climbs away through dense woodland, eventually rising to a junction where a side path is signed to Thor's Cave. It rises steeply to the cavern's yawning entrance, from which there is a magnificent view back along the valley. Archaeological excavations have revealed that it was inhabited during prehistoric times, a haven offering both shelter and security.

Turn as if to retrace your steps, but immediately bear right on a path that contours around the rock to a gate. Keep ahead along the undulating boundary of sloping fields, shortly reaching a wall stile out onto the end of an enclosed track. Follow it left towards Wetton. Meeting a lane, walk right, almost immediately going right again at a junction. Turn left at the end to return to the car park. ●

Bear right along the escarpment, passing through a gap in the corner of a broken wall to descend to a narrow gate. Proceed downhill past more mine workings, turning the corner in front of a stone building, built in 1788 to house a steam engine designed by James Watt. The way continues straight down the ever-steepening hill bringing you to a wall at the bottom, which is crossed by a stile at its right-hand end. Turn right to pass beneath an arch abutting the whimsical house seen from the top of the hill and follow a track out to the lane by Dale Bridge. Cross the lane as if to go over the bridge, but turn off left just before it through a gate onto the Manifold Track **C**.

Created in 1937 by Staffordshire County Council, the path follows the disused Leek and Manifold Light Railway. The single-track line carried mainly milk and also a few tourists, but enjoyed only a brief existence between 1904 and 1934. Its course now provides a splendid passage for cyclists and walkers and as you follow the winding river, it is easy to see how the

A Five Dales Walk

		GPS waypoints
Start	Tideswell	
Distance	6¾ miles (10.9km)	🥾 SK 152 757
Height gain	1,250 feet (381m)	Ⓐ SK 165 751
Approximate time	3½ hours	Ⓑ SK 175 744
Parking	Roadside parking in village	Ⓒ SK 173 727
Route terrain	Field and woodland paths, the	Ⓓ SK 157 731
	flood diversion ends in a brief but	Ⓔ SK 154 745
	awkward clamber	
Ordnance Survey maps	Landranger 119 (Buxton & Matlock), Explorer OL24	
	(The Peak District – White Peak area)	

The five dales featured here are: Tansley, Cressbrook, Water-cum-Jolly, Miller's and Tideswell, each attractive and having a distinctive character. The walk begins at a fine church known as the 'Cathedral of the Peak' built on the wealth derived from wool and lead. There is evidence too of former industrial activity along the banks of the Wye in the imposing water-powered mills at Cressbrook and Litton, although today it is once again Nature that holds sway in the dales.

Tideswell is one of those places that is difficult to categorise – for although barely larger than a village, it has all the bustle and appearance of a lively town. Tideswell developed during the later part of the Middle Ages as an important market and lead-mining centre and its imposing church, justifiably dubbed the 'Cathedral of the Peak', was built during its heyday. Dedicated to St John the Baptist, it is predominantly a 14th-century building with a fine porch and tall, pinnacled west tower. Unusually for a village church, it has two transepts. Inside, it is spacious and dignified with old tombs and ornate 19th-century wood carving that would put many a parish church in much larger towns to shame. With the decline of the mining industry, the place faded into relative obscurity, leaving

the church to remind us of its prosperous past.

🥾 Begin from the church, crossing the road to turn right. At a fork in front of the bank, branch left along Church Street, following that for 50 yds before turning left up a narrow passage at the end of the first terrace of houses. Climb steps at the back to a track above the houses and follow it left out to a lane. To the right, it leads over the hill to Litton, ¾ mile away. Meeting the main road, go left through the village, its 17th- and 18th-century stone cottages set back behind broad grass verges. Towards the far end, just beyond a cream-painted house with a decorated façade, a footpath sign directs you right towards a farmyard at the rear Ⓐ.

At the entrance, beside a cottage, cross a stile on the left from which a

Cressbrook Mill has been restored as residential apartments

path is signed to Cressbrook Dale and Wardlow. Strike across the field to a walled track at the far side. A few yards to the left, is a stile on the right. Walk down the narrow field, curving around the bottom-left wall corner and dropping to another stile. Beyond, a path falls past the pockmarks of old mine workings, following the deepening gorge of Tansley Dale to its junction with Cressbrook Dale. Over a stile at the bottom, sturdy stepping stones provide an occasionally necessary crossing of the streambed, then turn right. Almost immediately, the path forks, the higher branch rising determinedly past a fenced mine shaft to the top of the eastern flank of the valley ❸. *You can alternatively stay with the path along the valley floor, although the climb is amply rewarded by a splendid view along the dale with the cottages and farms of Litton still visible on the horizon.*

Beyond the viewpoint, the upper path immediately slopes back into the dale, dropping through coppiced woodland to rejoin the bottom track. A little farther on, the path crosses a footbridge then twists left into bushes. Immediately leave the path to climb steeply beside a wall at the edge of trees. As the gradient eases, keep ahead across the grass, from where there is a view to the almost

perpendicular cliffs enclosing the other side of the dale. A track develops, which leads on through a wood, shortly emerging onto a lane. Follow it downhill to Cressbrook where, just before the perimeter walls of the converted mill, a concessionary path is signed off on the right to Litton Mill ❸.

Skirt the rear of Cressbrook Mill, which was built in 1815, but more recently became almost derelict before it was developed as a housing complex. The path turns away beside the old leat that once fed the waterwheels to a junction below the expansive millpond. Bear right, crossing the leat to follow a path around the back of the pond beneath a high overhanging limestone cliff, a favourite practice ground for rock climbers. Continue upstream beside the River Wye through the delightful and oddly named Water-cum-Jolly Dale.

A flooding river may occasionally render the path beneath the cliff impassable. In which case, return to the road, Point ❸, go left and immediately fork left to climb steeply away. After some 200 yds, just beyond the last house, slip through a gap in the left wall. Contour the wooded bank above the cliffs to pass below Cressbrook Hall. The path then descends the steepening slope back into trees, finishing in a short clamber to rejoin the main path.

As the river narrows, the valley becomes Miller's Dale, the path passing the remains of one of its old mills. It is a lovely place, where the steep grassy meadows above fall to sheer cliffs that enclose the swift flowing river and a bordering strip of wetland wood. Eventually reaching Litton Mill, which, like Cressbrook, has been renovated for accommodation, the way winds across the tailrace to climb between the factory and mill-workers' cottages. Carry on for a further $^{1}/_{4}$ mile along a lane, quitting it where a track forks off right, just before a small parking area **D**.

Signed Tideswell Dale, the path follows a twisting, babbling brook, first on one bank and then crossing a little higher up. The dale is of a very different character to the others explored on the walk, well wooded and having a very gentle complexion. Towards the top, formal paths have been laid on both sides of the stream, rejoining to lead to a car park. Walk through and continue on a path parallel to the road beside a magnificent row of mature beech trees. Joining the road at its end, cross and go right, leaving along another path just beyond a small water treatment plant **E**.

The path climbs to the right across the sloping hillside, shortly meeting a track. Walk right to reach a lane and drop back to the main road at the edge of the village. The church from which the walk began stands at the far end. ●

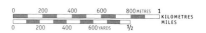

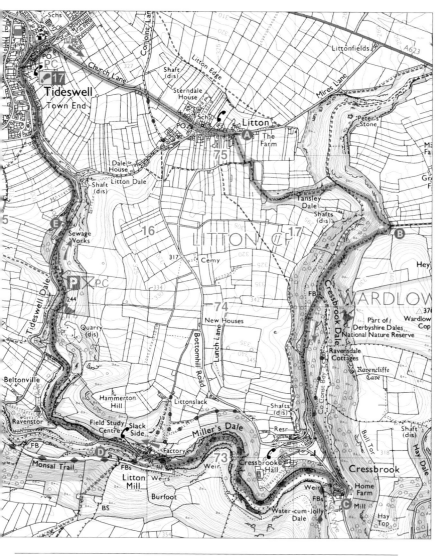

Cromford and Matlock Bath

		GPS waypoints
Start	Cromford Wharf	⬚ SK 299 570
Distance	7 miles (11.3km)	Ⓐ SK 300 572
Height gain	1,390 feet (424m)	Ⓑ SK 300 586
Approximate time	3½ hours	Ⓒ SK 297 583
Parking	Pay and Display at start	Ⓓ SK 293 580
Route terrain	Woodland paths and tracks, narrow lane	Ⓔ SK 295 569
		Ⓕ SK 298 561
Ordnance Survey maps	Landranger 119 (Buxton & Matlock), Explorer OL24 (The Peak District – White Peak area)	Ⓖ SK 293 557
		Ⓗ SK 313 559

An incredible variety of scenic and historic attractions are packed into this absorbing walk. The natural wonders include the narrow Derwent gorge and the impressive Black Rock above Cromford. Equally striking is the Victorian architecture of Matlock Bath, the fascinating mill settlement of Cromford and the railway incline dropping to the Cromford Canal, where the former workshops house an interesting museum.

In 1771 Sir Richard Arkwright, a Lancashire cotton entrepreneur, established the first successful water-powered cotton mill in the then scattered farming community of Cromford – an event which helped transform textile manufacturing from a cottage-based craft into a factory-located industry. Arkwright chose Cromford because of the power of the River Derwent, but it did have two disadvantages: a shortage of labour and poor communications. He created a village to bring people from the surrounding countryside, but the second difficulty was never completely overcome. Although he built a canal, which was later linked by railway to the Peak Forest Canal at Whaley Bridge, Cromford was far from the sea ports through which raw cotton and finished goods were traded. Unable to compete effectively with the main centres of the

On top of Black Rock

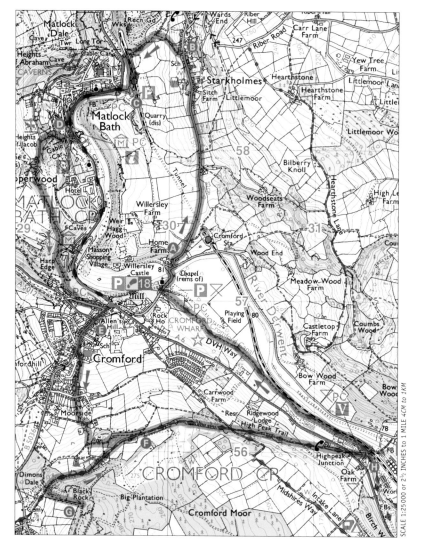

SCALE 1:25000 or 2½ INCHES to 1 MILE 4CM to 1KM

cotton industry, the town never developed into another Manchester or Bolton. However, what remains is a rare example of an early Industrial Revolution textile settlement, which has retained many of the original buildings erected by Arkwright and his successors. Some of these can be found near the start of the walk, which begins at the head of the canal opposite Arkwright's Mill. The complex dates from the late 18th century and is being restored by the Arkwright Society.

Turn right past the church, founded towards the end of the 18th century as a private chapel for the Arkwrights and where Sir Richard was buried. It was enlarged in the 19th century to accommodate the growing community. Across the bridge is the entrance to Willersley Castle, once home to the industrialist and now a hotel. Fork left just past there up a steep lane to Starkholmes **Ⓐ**; be aware of traffic for the lane is narrow and has no footway. Where it later levels, a fine view opens across the valley to Matlock Bath. Reaching the village, look for a footpath on the left, just before the **White Lion** ⓑ.

Doubling back, wind down the hillside, joining another path at the edge of a wood. Beyond the Heights of Abraham cable car station, pass beneath a railway bridge and turn left beside the river to a bridge opposite Matlock Bath Station ⓒ.

The arrival of the railway helped Matlock Bath develop as a popular spar, bringing Victorians to take the waters in the Pavilion and Pump Room and enjoy the riverside gardens and scenery, still appreciated today.

Follow the main road left to the Pavilion, crossing to a footpath beside the **Fishpond pub** ⓓ. At the top go right past the entrance to the Gulliver's World Theme Park, leaving just beyond where a path is signed left to Upperwood. Briefly join the theme park's rising drive, but leave in a few yards for another path on the right. After 100 yds, turn left onto a stepped path that climbs the steep hillside to emerge onto a lane.

Go left through the hamlet of Upperwood, bearing left at a fork. Beyond the houses keep ahead as the way degrades to a track and then a footpath, a signpost directing you towards Scarthin. The ongoing path falls gradually across a wooded hillside, where in spring you will find celandine, wood anemone, wood sorrel and ransom. Lower down, keep ahead and then bear right at consecutive junctions, passing behind a large hotel. Beside the road far below is Masson Mill, begun by Sir Richard Arkwright in 1783-4.

The path shortly curves across the rib of the hill, zigzagging down the opposite flank to emerge in the former lead-mining settlement of Scarthin. Walk left through the village to the main road ⓔ.

Turn up the hill in the direction of Cromford, passing North Street. Built in 1776 to accommodate Arkwright's workforce, the three-storey terraces are regarded as Britain's earliest planned industrial housing and were greatly in advance of their time. Continue for another 200 yds to find a narrow alley on the left, Beedhouse Lane, which then curves right behind house gardens. Meeting a street, the ongoing track opposite is signed to Black Rock. At the top of that, walk left on a narrow lane. Bend right and then go left at the next junction, continuing beyond a house on a grass track into a wood. Through a gate, a path winds past a disused quarry before ending at a couple of stiles. Clamber over the one on the right to gain the old trackbed of the former Cromford and High Peak Railway ⓕ.

Black Rock lies $^1/_2$ mile (800m) to the right. Reaching a car park, take a path on the left. It climbs to the top of the impressive outcrop of weatherworn gritstone boulders from which there is a splendid panoramic view across the countryside ⓖ.

Descend and go back along the railway, continuing beyond ⓕ to pass the old winding house at Sheep Pasture. It was built in 1830 to haul wagons up and down the $^3/_4$ mile (1.2km) 1 in 8 incline to High Peak Junction beside the Cromford Canal. At the end of the track, the restored workshops in the marshalling yard house an interesting museum. Cross a canal bridge to join the towpath ⓗ.

If you have the time, a short walk to the right takes you to the Leawood Pump House, built in 1849 to lift water from the River Derwent into the Cromford Canal. The return, however, is to the left, a pleasant one-mile stroll beside the waterway back to Cromford Wharf. ●

Chrome Hill

Start	Longnor	**GPS waypoints**	
Distance	7 miles (11.3km)	 SK 088 649	
Height gain	1,500 feet (457m)	Ⓐ SK 081 661	
Approximate time	3½ hours	Ⓑ SK 076 670	
Parking	In the village square	Ⓒ SK 064 682	
Route terrain	Field and rocky paths. *Special care needed on the narrow, exposed ridges of Chrome and Parkhouse hills*	Ⓓ SK 076 678	
		Ⓔ SK 082 677	
		Ⓕ SK 084 670	
		Ⓖ SK 082 669	
		Ⓗ SK 083 665	
Ordnance Survey maps	Landranger 119 (Buxton & Matlock), Explorer OL24 (The Peak District – White Peak area)	Ⓙ SK 095 659	

If the culmination of gritstone landscapes is found along its dramatic edges, then the limestone equivalent surely lies here, where a couple of soaring reef knolls rise to knife-sharp ridges above the infant River Dove. The route picks a way over one and gives an opportunity to scale the other as well as taking in some of the attractive dry gorges that split this frontier land between the dark and white rocks.

The walk begins from Longnor village square, overlooked by **pubs**, a **tearoom** and the 19th-century Market Hall, still boasting a board detailing the tolls. Take the winding alleyway to the left of the hall, Chapel Street and at the top, go left into Church Street. Just before the main road, swing right into a narrow lane. Abandon it after 100 yds for a path on the right, winding past houses to continue at the field edge. Over a stile, descend left through scrub, joining a track at the bottom from Underhill Farm. Approaching a cottage, bear right along a lesser track. Keep left past Yewtree Grange before rising once more to meet the road.

Go right for some 250 yds, leaving along the second of adjacent tracks on the left Ⓐ. Approaching a gate, branch left on a signed path above a house. Continue over a stile and

Chrome Hill presents a dramatic profile from across the valley

lose height to a footbridge across the nascent River Dove. Maintain the line to a lane skirting Parkhouse Hill. Go left and then keep right at a fork, shortly reaching a cattle-grid **B**.

Quit the lane over a stile on the left, from which a path, signed High Edge via Chrome Hill attacks the steep ridge. Stick to the crest, crossing a stile beneath a sturdy sycamore part-way up, where a pause is justified to admire the view back to the adjacent Parkhouse Hill. Unmitigated, the ascent continues to the summit, from which there is an unrivalled panorama to the upper Dove valley and northern moors.

The name of the hill has nothing to do with chromite, the ore from which metallic chrome is obtained. Instead, pronounced 'croom', it derives from the Old English 'crump' meaning curved or crooked, an apt epithet for the humped spine of the hill. Chrome Hill and its craggy neighbours are the remnants of a coral reef that grew in a shallow Carboniferous tropical sea and the spectacularly ragged summit is dotted with bare outcrops, caves, hollows and arches that once provided shelter for undersea life. The top is exposed and, as the ground falls almost sheer on both sides, a good head for heights is needed. *Care is particularly required in high wind and in wet weather, when both grass and rock are slippery.*

The descent is equally abrupt and leads to a stile. Continue beside a fence to a second stile and then climb to leave at the top-left corner of the rising enclosure. Accompany the right-hand wall to a metalled track above Stoop Farm **C**.

Follow it over a cattle-grid to a junction and go right again, the narrow lane wandering across open hillsides above Greensides into the head of Dowel Dale. The now-dry valley was an underwater channel between the reefs and on the left is a cave known as Owl

Hole. Where the confined gorge later swings right, leave through a wicket gate on the left **D**. A trod picks its way up the steep hillside to another gate in the top wall. Head out parallel to a stone boundary to the left, crossing a stile beside a field gate to continue with a wall then on the right. About 100 yds before its end, look for a stile onto the adjacent track **E**.

Cross to another stile opposite and head into the fold of a small valley, which leads down to Glutton Grange. Through a gate, go left, but approaching the farmhouse, swing right around the end barn **F**. Leave the yard over a stile on the left and turn right to a gate beside a water trough. Continue to the top corner of a linear enclosure, twisting through a couple of small gates onto the access land of Parkhouse Hill **G**.

*You now have the option to scale the Parkhouse ridge. Although somewhat lower than Chrome, the climb is equally steep to and from the exposed ridge, which is even narrower and definitely unsuitable for those with a tendency to suffer from vertigo. The high route drops to the lane at Point **B**, which you should then follow left back below the hill.* Alternatively, you can avoid the

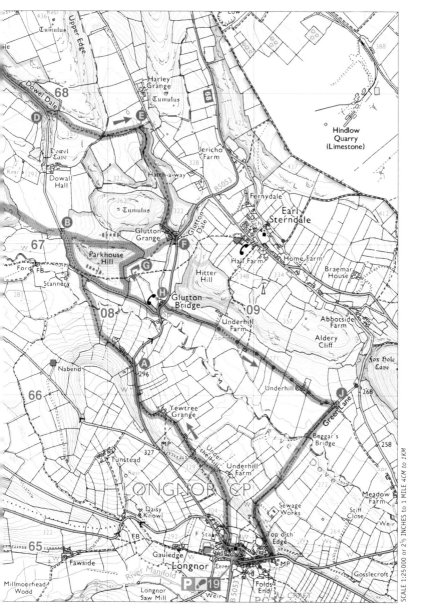

SCALE 1:25 000 or 2½ INCHES to 1 MILE 4CM to 1KM

climb by simply following the wall left over the low shoulder. Drop to the lane by a cattle-grid and go left to the main road at Glutton Bridge. Turn left again before shortly leaving along a track on the right **H**.

Keep ahead, later passing a cottage and continuing at the edge of fields to a farm, Underhill. Carry on until the track swings sharply left **J**, there turning right through a gate along a grass track to a bridge across the Dove. Head over a rise, crossing a couple of marshy streams beyond and making progress at the field edge to reach a barn. Exit onto the adjacent concrete track and follow it uphill to cottages at Top o' th' Edge. Walk down to meet the road at the edge of Longnor and follow it right, back into the village. ●

Three Shire Heads and Axe Edge Moor

		GPS waypoints
Start	Cat and Fiddle Inn	
Distance	7¼ miles (11.7km)	🖉 SK 000 718
Height gain	1,080 feet (329m)	Ⓐ SK 009 700
		Ⓑ SK 009 685
Approximate time	3½ hours	Ⓒ SK 020 687
Parking	Roadside parking opposite pub	Ⓓ SK 026 703
		Ⓔ SK 027 713
Route terrain	Generally clear moorland paths, care needed in mist	
Ordnance Survey maps	Landranger 118 (Stoke-on-Trent & Macclesfield), Explorer OL24 (The Peak District – White Peak area)	

*In poor weather, the moorland summit of the Macclesfield –
Buxton road can appear bleak and uninviting, but a brighter
complexion reveals panoramic views across a spacious landscape
variously carpeted in heather and cotton grass. Meandering the
remote folds and edges of Axe Edge Moor, the route leads to
Three Shire Heads, a beautiful spot where streams and paths
meet at an ancient packhorse bridge on which the counties of
Cheshire, Staffordshire and Derbyshire converge.*

At 1,690 feet (516m) the **Cat and Fiddle**
is the second highest inn in England,
beaten only by the Tan Hill Inn in the
northern Pennines. It was built to serve
the turnpike road completed in 1823,
which was later superseded by the
present main road. Not surprisingly, it is
a popular haven for walkers, cyclists
and motorists alike.

🖉 With your back to the inn, take
the track opposite across open moorland.
Beginning from such a high altitude
there are immediately impressive views
across the Cheshire plain while to the
south west, the distinctive peak of
Shutlingsloe rises above Wildboarclough.
After gently climbing, keep on with the
main track at a junction, signed to
Three Shires Heads. It falls through
Danebower Hollow, eventually meeting

the main A54 Ⓐ. Walk right, doubling
back after 200 yds along a gated track.
In 100 yds, at the end of the
accompanying fence, drop steeply past
a lone chimney to a grassy path below.
To the right it follows the meandering
course of the infant River Dane, before
long leading to a bridge across a side
stream. Carry on along the valley for a
further ¼ mile to a stone bridge across
the Dane at Three Shire Heads Ⓑ.

It is a lovely spot at the confluence of
confined, steep-sided and bracken-
covered valleys, where two lively
streams, each spanned by a narrow
packhorse bridge, tumble over rocky
falls to mingle their waters. Just below
is Panniers Pool, taking its name from
the large baskets in which the pack
animals carried their heavy loads. The

place was perhaps the site of a ford before the bridges were built, or it may merely have been somewhere that the horses were taken down to the water to drink.

Turn over the first bridge and then walk ahead through a gate to gain height beside the tributary stream. Where the way later levels at a junction, bear left, sticking with the stream towards Orchard Common. Emerging through a gate onto a tarmac track by the entrance to Black Clough Farm, keep ahead up the hill, before long reaching a right-hand bend **G**. Fork left

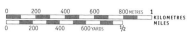

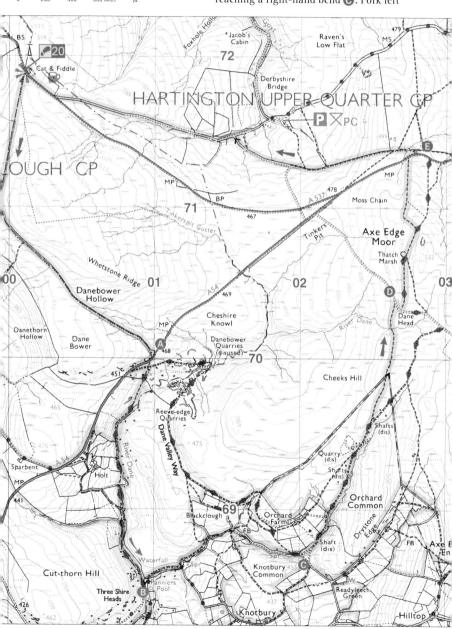

onto a track, which drops over a bridge before climbing away in a steady ascent. Go forward as the track bends to Orchard Farm, passing through a gate to continue on a broad path rising beside the clough. After ¹/₂ mile, just beyond overgrown spoil heaps standing above to the left, look for a small concrete stump hidden in the grass on the right, which marks an abandoned mine shaft. There, bear left on a rising trod across the moor to the corner of a wall breaking the skyline. Crossing a stile, carry on in the same direction, eventually meeting a lane at Dane Head **D**.

Go right, but then almost immediately swing left onto a broad grassy path that heads away across the stark expanses of Axe Edge Moor. To the east, the ground rises to over 1,800 feet (549m) before abruptly falling over the gritstone escarpment of Axe Edge, which overlooks Buxton as well as a good slice of the Peak District. The moor is a major watershed and five rivers; the Dove, Manifold, Wye, Derwent and Goyt, all begin their journey to the sea from its peaty slopes.

As the way crests, look for a narrower path splitting off on the left. It drops away before curving right, ultimately bringing you to the main A54 road **E**. Cross right and double back left on a path beside a fence and broken wall. There are fine views to the right into the head of the Goyt Valley, while to the front, at the top of the hill is the **Cat and Fiddle Inn**. Meeting the corner of a lane, keep going into the valley. At the bottom, turn left and climb once more back to the main road, joining it just short of your starting point. ●

Across Axe Edge Moor to the Goyt Valley

Baslow and Curbar edges

		GPS waypoints	
Start	Baslow	🖉	SK 258 722
Distance	7¼ miles (11.7km)	Ⓐ	SK 256 724
Height gain	1,140 feet (347m)	Ⓑ	SK 262 736
Approximate time	3½ hours	Ⓒ	SK 249 762
Parking	Pay and Display at start	Ⓓ	SK 243 760
Route terrain	Generally clear paths and tracks throughout	Ⓔ	SK 244 753
		Ⓕ	SK 247 744
Ordnance Survey maps	Landranger 119 (Buxton & Matlock), Explorer OL24 (The Peak District – White Peak area)	Ⓖ	SK 251 745

A magnificent gritstone escarpment stretches along the eastern rim of the Derwent Valley from Birchen Edge northwards to Derwent Edge, providing both exhilarating walking and glorious views. This ramble traverses Baslow Edge and Curbar Edge, two of the finest sections of this long cliff. Plunging through thick woods to the banks of the Derwent, it returns along the riverbank and across fields to Baslow.

The rather suburbanised and strung-out village of Baslow lies at the northern end of Chatsworth Park and near the southern limit of the long line of gritstone edges, which occupy a frontier position above the River Derwent between the limestone of the White Peak and the gritstone of the Dark Peak.

🖉 Out of the car park, cross to the main road and take the uphill street opposite, Eaton Hill. Where it later bends past a small triangular green, turn right to head up Bar Road Ⓐ. Beyond the last of the houses, the road degrades to a rough track winding up the hill. Through a gate at its end, keep climbing onto the moor until you reach a fork Ⓑ. A little distance to the right, occupying a splendid vantage above the valley is the Wellington Monument, erected in 1866. On the opposite side of the valley above Gardom's Edge, sharp eyes will spot another monument to the

memory of Nelson.

The onward route, however, lies to the left, soon passing a massive isolated rock, the Eagle Stone. Its name is supposedly a corruption of Egglestone, meaning Witches Stone. Tradition had it that before a local lad could marry, he had to prove his worth (and curry the favour of the witch) by scaling the 20-foot (6m) high rock. Negotiating the many overhangs was no easy task and one wonders how many bachelors it created.

The main track carries on for a further ½ mile to a gate, but for the best views across the Derwent Valley, take one of the lesser paths to the left that wander along the rim of Baslow Edge. Through the gate, cross a lane and continue onto Curbar Edge. The weathered outcrops of gritstone here are truly impressive, the massive boulders, buttresses and pillars lining the sheer escarpment a haunt for rock climbers. Follow the edge for a little over a mile until you meet a walled enclosure. Immediately before it, a narrower path forks left, dropping to a shelf beneath the precipitous cliffs. About 100 yds along, and prior to reaching a detached pillar, look for a less-obvious rocky path that doubles back steeply into the woods below **C**.

The gradient shortly eases, the path weaving between the trees to a gate. Continue through the wood to a road by the **Chequers Inn**. Cross to a stile opposite and keep ahead, descending across a meadow and then open woodland. Emerging onto a lane at the bottom, follow it right to Froggatt Bridge. Turn over the bridge but then immediately leave by a stone stile on the left **D**.

A riverside path, signed to New Bridge and Calver, winds through a conifer plantation and on at the edge of successive tree-fringed meadows, eventually meeting a lane at New Bridge **E**. Cross to a track opposite

Curbar Edge offers some amazing viewpoints

passing cottages above a weir and continue along a wooded path beside The Goit, which carried water to power the mill at Calver. Breaking from the trees, move away from the leat towards Stocking Farm and leave along a track to the road. Recross the river on the bridge, from where there is a glimpse of the fine, early 19th-century Calver Mill. Its forbidding appearance made it an ideal substitute for Colditz Castle in the 1970s television series. Carry on to a junction opposite the **Bridge Inn** **F**.

Take the second of the two lanes on the left, Curbar Lane, beside the church, and follow it steeply uphill for ¼ mile. At a crossroads by a telephone box **G**, turn right into Cliff Lane. Just beyond a bend and the crest of the hill, a path over a stile on the left is signed to Baslow via Gorse Bank Farm. Pass between house gardens and continue towards Lane Farm, crossing a stile below the buildings to follow an old walled path down between the fields.

Keep going beyond its end to a gate, through which curve left to join a wall on the right. Reaching adjacent gates, pass through the one on the left and climb across a field to the top corner above another farm. Go right to a gate-gap and then ahead beside a fence. Through another gap bear left across the next enclosure, passing through a third gap and on to a squeeze stile by a gate. The track ahead leads to Gorse Bank Farm. Continue through the yard and follow Gorsebank Lane gently downhill for ½ mile to the edge of Baslow. Reaching a junction, turn right into Bar Road

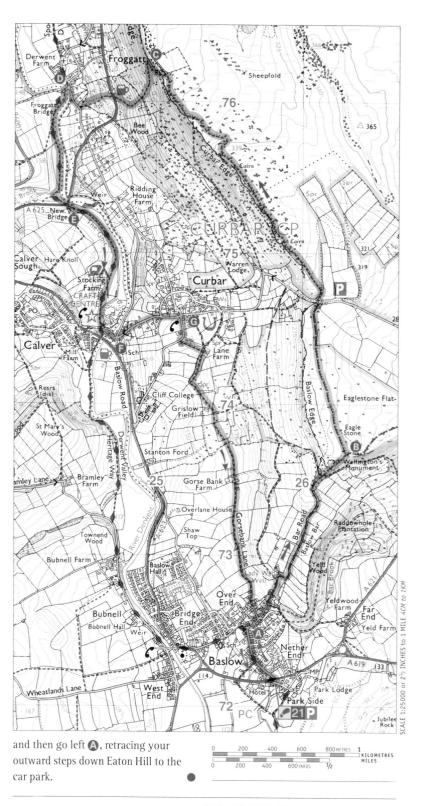

and then go left **A**, retracing your
outward steps down Eaton Hill to the
car park.

Beresford and Wolfscote dales

Start	Hartington	
Distance	8 miles (12.9km)	
Height gain	1,360 feet (415m)	
Approximate time	4 hours	
Parking	In village	
Route terrain	Paths, tracks and field trods, steep grassy descent	
Ordnance Survey maps	Landranger 119 (Buxton & Matlock), Explorer OL24 (The Peak District – White Peak area)	

GPS waypoints

- 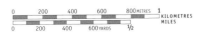 SK 128 604
- Ⓐ SK 128 586
- Ⓑ SK 126 576
- Ⓒ SK 126 566
- Ⓓ SK 126 564
- Ⓔ SK 134 556
- Ⓕ SK 145 561
- Ⓖ SK 130 584
- Ⓗ SK 133 596

After its wide valley north of Hartington, the River Dove flows through the gorge-like Beresford and Wolfscote dales. Many declare these dales to be as equally attractive as Dovedale proper and this superlatively beautiful ramble includes two of the loveliest Peak District villages, some sweeping views and long stretches of glorious riverside walking through the dales themselves.

Like a number of Peak villages, Hartington was once a bustling centre, and the limestone houses, **inns** and shops grouped attractively around the spacious market place have the atmosphere more of a small town than a village. Dominated by a large and handsome medieval church, the village occupies a grand setting about ¹⁄₂ mile from the river above its narrowing into Beresford Dale.

From the market place, take the B5054 road towards Warslow, leaving left after some 150 yds for a footpath between Rooke's Pottery and the **public conveniences**, set back from the road. Signed to Beresford and Wolfscote Dales, it leads to a field behind, swinging right past a cottage and on by a wall. Through a gate, cross a track into the next field, the view ahead

inviting you into a lush and gentle wooded landscape. Slipping through a gap in a wall, maintain your direction and, beyond a gate, skirt the base of a low, conical hill. The way continues through a small wood to emerge beside the River Dove. The area is associated with the famous angler Izaak Walton, who wrote *The Compleat Angler* in 1676. He frequently fished this part of the river in the company of his friend Charles Cotton, who lived at nearby Beresford Hall. The hall was demolished in 1858, but the 17th-century 'fishing temple' survives. The path shortly crosses a footbridge by Pike Pool, so called by Charles Cotton, not for the fish but after the thin spire of rock that

0	200	400	600	800 METRES	1
					KILOMETRES
					MILES
0	200	400	600 YARDS	¹⁄₂	

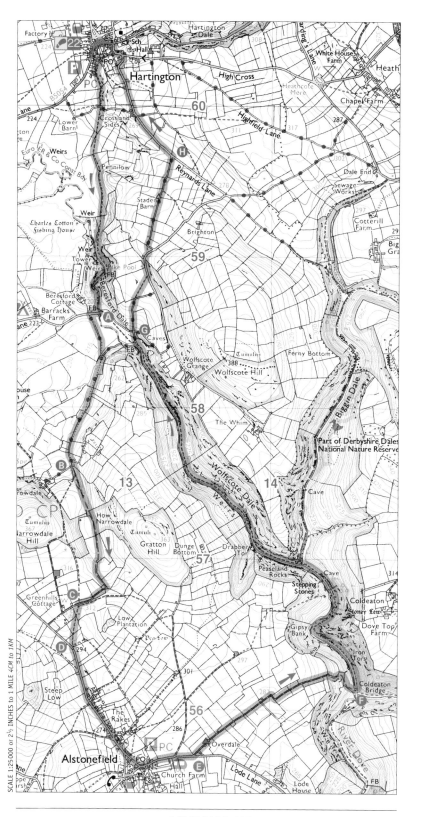

Above Alstonefield

towers above the river. Carry on through Beresford Dale, ignoring a second bridge at its end to turn out onto the end of a lane **Ⓐ**.

Walk from the river, but after 50 yds turn left through a gate. Signed as a cycle route to Hartington, the track hugs the field edge. Keep ahead where the cycle path later leaves left, continuing through a succession of gates for almost ³/₄ mile and eventually rising to a sharp right turn **Ⓑ**. Go forward through a gate along a gently rising grassy fold, appropriately called Narrowdale, and carry on beyond another gate, joining a wall on your right into the broader upper valley. Shortly pick up another wall on your left, pausing at the top corner to enjoy the retrospective view before turning right to a gate and stile. Follow a walled track over the crest, shortly reaching an intersecting path indicated by a four-way signpost **Ⓒ**. Pass through the kissing-gate on the left and, guided by a sign to Alstonefield, bear right across the pasture to another gate at the corner of a small wood. Maintain the diagonal across the resultant fields to emerge onto a lane **Ⓓ**.

Turn left into Alstonefield, a delightfully unspoiled and peaceful village standing 900 feet (274m) on a plateau between the Dove and Manifold valleys. Grey stone cottages are grouped around a charming green and village inn, while its lovely old church can be found along a lane, just to the south. Although dating mostly from the 14th and 15th centuries, it retains a Norman doorway and chancel arch and contains the family pew formerly used by the Cottons from nearby Beresford Hall.

Approaching the village centre go left and then left again at successive junctions, following signs to Lode Mill and Ashbourne. After ¹/₄ mile turn off along the second of two tracks on the left, signed to the Youth Hostel and Coldeaton Bridge via Gipsy Bank **Ⓔ**. It later doglegs right and left, becoming narrower and ultimately ending at a stile. The onward path drops right to the head of a shallow gully, following it sharply down to Coldeaton Bridge spanning the River Dove below **Ⓕ**.

Cross the bridge and turn left, accompanying the river through Wolfscote Dale, a sinuous steep-sided gorge, thickly wooded at first, but later opening to smooth grassy slopes broken by spectacular limestone crags. Keep going for almost two miles past Gipsy Bank Bridge to Frank i' th' Rocks Bridge **Ⓖ**. Remaining on this bank, leave the river along an uphill track, continuing across a junction to a right-hand bend at the top of the hill. Go forward over a stile and bear right, crossing the field to a wall stile somewhat short of the far corner. *(Note that between April and July, you are asked to divert around the perimeter track to the lane.)* Joining the lane, follow it left and around a bend, leaving soon after along a track signed left to Hartington. Very shortly swinging right, it falls in a straight gentle descent to Reynards Lane **Ⓗ**. Walk down the hill towards the village, going left and left again when you reach the main road to return to the market place.　　●

Macclesfield Forest and the 'Cheshire Matterhorn'

		GPS waypoints	
Start	Wildboarclough		SJ 986 699
Distance	7¾ miles (12.5km)	**A**	SJ 981 713
Height gain	1,770 feet (540m)	**B**	SJ 985 719
Approximate time	4 hours	**C**	SJ 979 722
Parking	Car park at Clough House	**D**	SJ 971 722
Route terrain	Upland pasture and forest paths, a steep initial descent off Shutlingsloe	**E**	SJ 962 726
		F	SJ 952 715
		G	SJ 956 710
		H	SJ 976 695
Ordnance Survey maps	Landranger 118 (Stoke-on-Trent & Macclesfield), Explorer OL24 (The Peak District – White Peak area)	**J**	SJ 982 690

From a distance it is easy to see why Shutlingsloe has been described as the 'Cheshire Matterhorn', for although only rising to 1,659 feet, its abrupt and distinctive peak bears a striking resemblance to its Continental counterpart. Much of this ramble is across the former royal hunting domain of Macclesfield Forest, a sparsely populated area of isolated farms, rolling hills, wild moorlands and rushing streams. The area has seen little change over the centuries, apart from the planting of conifers and the construction of reservoirs on its western perimeter. For most of the way this is an undulating route but towards the end there is a long, though not particularly steep or strenuous climb to the summit of Shutlingsloe, followed by a short, sharp descent.

Macclesfield Forest comprises a number of plantations occupying the western slopes of the Peak District overlooking the Cheshire plain. It is just a small part of what, in the Middle Ages, was a large, royal hunting forest, much of which would have been as it is today, open moorland rather than thick woodland.

From the northern end of the car park, turn right along the lane. After a mile, just past a turning to Forest Chapel, leave along a farm track on the right **A**. Over a stream, but before a cattle-grid, go left onto another track rising beside Clough Brook. Reaching a cottage and barns at the end, wend left through a gate to a bridge spanning the stream. Continue briefly along the opposite bank of the stream, before moving left through an open gateway **B**, from which a contained broad grass track swings left up the hill.

After gaining height beside a ruined building and old walls, it veers right past a stepped stile on the left. Cross that and strike right up the hillside to

another stile beside a gate at the top corner. Beyond, follow a descending wall. Approaching the corner, look for a stone stile and cross to continue down on the other flank of the wall. Pass through a gate at the bottom corner and carry on to a bridge over a stream. Bear left up to a gate onto a lane beside the entrance to a house **C**.

Go left and then immediately right at a junction, the climbing lane signed to Forest Chapel. After some 100 yds, turn right onto an old, sunken track that rises over the hill to the chapel. This plain and simple church, built in 1673 and reconstructed in 1831, is in total harmony with the surroundings. The church is one of several where a rush-bearing ceremony is held to commemorate the annual renewal of the rushes that originally covered most church floors.

At a junction just past the church, take a track on the right, which soon leads to the edge of a forest plantation **D**. Leave the track through a gate on the left from which a clear path winds away among the trees. After $\frac{1}{2}$ mile, the way falls more steeply to reach a junction in a partial clearing before a ruined barn **E**.

Signed to Langley, the track left resumes an easy descent through the forest. Eventually joining a tarmac lane, the more open ground to the right affords a view to the bold crags of Tegg's Nose. Carry on to a junction in front of a pub, **Leather's Smithy F**.

Immediately past the merging lane, leave through a squeeze gap beside a gate on the left, onto a grass track below Ridgegate Reservoir. At the far side, by a sign to Shutlingsloe, bear left, dipping to cross another dam. Keeping right, climb away from the water. Swinging left at the top, follow a track out to the corner of a lane. Walk ahead a little way to find a gated entrance to the forest on the right **G**.

Instead of taking the main bridlepath, go through a small gate to its left from which a footpath is signed to Shutlingsloe and Trentabank. After briefly shadowing the lane, it weaves down a wooded bank to meet a main forest track. Cross to the narrower path directly opposite. It winds up into the trees and before long meets another broad track. Picking up signs to

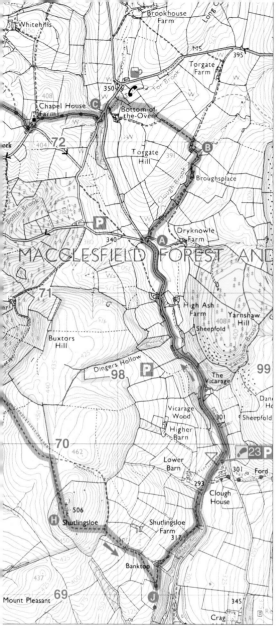

way briefly levels, the distinctive peak comes dramatically into view. Through a gate, turn beside the wall towards Shutlingsloe, soon crossing a stile for the final pull to the summit **H**.

Standing apart from the main body of hills, the spot affords a magnificent panorama on a clear day. To the north west is Macclesfield Forest and Tegg's Nose, while to the west the land falls away to the Cheshire plain. To the south are the Roaches above the Tittesworth Reservoir, while to the east the ground rises to the bleak expanse of Axe Edge Moor.

The route off is waymarked just beyond the trig point, a rocky path dropping steeply down the craggy face. Those with short legs will find the first section a bit of a scramble, but the gradient soon eases as the descent continues on the grass below. The obvious path lies over a couple of stiles before crossing a stream to join a tarmac drive. Follow it to the right, shortly reaching a cattle-grid **J**.

Double back left on a track above a wood, passing a cottage and barn to carry on along a grass path beside a wall. The way continues generally ahead over stiles and a small stream, finally ending at a lane. Follow it left back to the car park at Clough House. ●

Shutlingsloe once more, go right and then keep left when you meet another track. Reaching a junction in front of a gate, walk right, the way resuming a steady climb. Beyond another gate, ignore the first right, a bridleway, and continue a little farther to find a path signed off right to Shutlingsloe. Rising to a kissing-gate, leave the forest and carry on along a flagged path that gains height across the open hillside. As the

Ilam and Dovedale

Ilam and Dovedale

		GPS waypoints
Start	Dovedale	🖉 SK 146 509
Distance	8 miles (12.9km)	Ⓐ SK 135 508
Height gain	1,660 feet (506m)	Ⓑ SK 127 517
Approximate time	4 hours	Ⓒ SK 127 541
Parking	Pay and Display at southern end of Dovedale gorge	Ⓓ SK 139 546
		Ⓔ SK 151 513
Route terrain	Field paths and valley trails	
Ordnance Survey maps	Landranger 119 (Buxton & Matlock), Explorer OL24 (The Peak District – White Peak area)	

It is no wonder that so many visitors have enthused about Dovedale over the centuries, for by any standards it is supremely beautiful, one of the most delightful valleys in England. At a quiet time – a fine weekday in spring, autumn or even winter – this is a magical walk, across fields to the model estate village of Ilam and through the grounds of Ilam Hall by the River Manifold. After a climb to Stanshope and a descent to the hamlet of Milldale with splendid views into the valley of the Dove, there finally comes an enchanting walk beside the winding river, through the limestone ravine of Dovedale itself.

🖉 A sign opposite the main car park directs you through the overflow parking to Ilam and Alstonefield. Over a double stile at the back, head out behind the **Izaak Walton Hotel** across a succession of fields. As a track subsequently develops, drop left through a gate to emerge onto a lane. Walk right to a junction in the village by the memorial cross Ⓐ.

Ilam is essentially the creation of one man, the wealthy industrialist Jesse Watts Russell, who imitated some of his aristocratic contemporaries by remodelling his estate and re-siting the village. Russell rebuilt Ilam Hall during the 1820s in the Gothic style and then 30 years later relocated the village, adopting a picturesque, Alpine style that is unique in the Peak. In the centre

he erected an imitation Eleanor Cross in memory of his wife and restored the small 13th-century church, adding an octagonal and somewhat over-proportioned chapel to his father-in-law. The church is noted for its Saxon treasures: a font and two crosses in the churchyard and contains the tomb of St Bertram, a little-known 8th-century Mercian saint.

Turn right, but where the road then bends right, keep ahead towards the Country Park. Approaching the entrance, bear left and then go left again through a gate just before the entrance to Dovedale House to pass the church. Walk past the hall and climb steps to the terrace garden, from where there is a marvellous prospect back to Bunster Hill and Thorpe Cloud, the two hills that guard the entrance to Dovedale. Ilam Hall was partially demolished in the 1930s, but what was left, along with large areas of Dovedale, was given by Sir Robert McDougall to the National Trust. It now houses an information centre, shop and **tearoom**, whilst part is given over as a youth hostel.

Cross to a gate in the far corner, through which bear right, dropping between the trees to a path above the

River Manifold, known as Paradise Walk. To the right it leads shortly past the 'Battle Stone', the shaft of an 11th-century cross that was discovered in the foundations of a cottage during the rebuilding of Ilam. Its name derives from a popular association with local battles between the Anglo-Saxons and Vikings. Keep with the main path up the valley, which is delightfully wooded and eventually leads out beside a cottage onto a drive. Turn left over a cattle-grid to a fork Ⓑ.

The right branch rises along the valley to the fine old Castern Hall, winding around and behind it before gaining height once more to another farm, Castern, higher up the hill. Passing the cottage, leave over a stile beside a gate on the left and climb to a gap stile in the wall above, the way signed to Stanshope and Wetton. Turn right by the wall to a gate and go over a track to the field opposite. Head out, crossing an intervening fence before reaching a stile in a stone wall below. Negotiating that, turn left and walk at

the edge of successive fields. Ignoring the path left just before the fifth wall, cross the stile in front and bear left to the next stile. Beyond that, maintain the diagonal across a final field to emerge onto a lane. Go left towards the hamlet of Stanshope.

At a bend approaching Stanshope, turn off onto a walled track signed to Milldale and Dovedale Ⓒ. Towards the top of the hill the track turns right, but instead go forward through a gap stile beside a gate. Walk on at the edge of successive fields, the way eventually falling ever more steeply into a narrowing valley. Dropping through a gap past a cottage at the bottom, join a lane and follow it right to Milldale. At a junction in the hamlet go right again, passing a National Trust information barn to cross the narrow two-arched Viator's Bridge, which is mentioned by Izaak Walton in *The Compleat Angler,* his best-known work published in 1653 Ⓓ.

On the far bank, a well-made path follows the river downstream for $2\frac{1}{2}$ miles into Dovedale, its steep-sided and well-wooded gorge overhung with limestone crags, caves and pinnacles. Beyond Lover's Leap, a rocky outcrop affording superb views along the valley, the river flows below the crags of Dovedale Castle before turning abruptly below Thorpe Cloud, at which point stepping stones offer a way over the river Ⓔ.

You can either cross here or remain on this bank, walking beside the river for a further $\frac{1}{4}$ mile to a bridge. The car parks from which the walk began lie just a little farther downstream. ●

Stepping stones across the Dove

The Roaches and Lud's Church

		GPS waypoints
Start	Roaches Gate	✏ SK 004 621
Distance	8¼ miles (13.3km), shorter version 5¼ miles (8.4km)	Ⓐ SK 005 625
		Ⓑ SJ 995 644
Height gain	1,420 feet (433m)	Ⓒ SJ 977 655
Approximate time	4 hours, shorter version 2½ hours	Ⓓ SJ 995 645
Parking	Limited roadside parking at start. A weekend park and ride operates from nearby Tittesworth Reservoir	Ⓔ SK 012 632
Route terrain	Moorland paths	
Ordnance Survey maps	Landrangers 118 (Stoke-on-Trent & Macclesfield) and 119 (Buxton & Matlock), Explorer OL24 (The Peak District – White Peak area)	

The gritstone edge of The Roaches forms the dramatic western boundary of the Peak District, overlooking the lowlands of Staffordshire and Cheshire. It is an area of weirdly contorted rocks, which, together with the continuing ridge to the north, provide a magnificent three-mile (4.8km) high-level walk. The return lies across the shoulder of The Roaches past the equally intriguing outcrop Hen Cloud.

✏ Leave the lane at Roaches Gate to climb a broad, stony path making for the col between The Roaches and its near neighbour, Hen Cloud. The name 'Roaches' probably comes from the French 'roche', meaning 'rock'. Take the second path off to the left, which passes below a stone building and Rockhall Cottage, once a gamekeeper's cottage and now the Don Whillans Memorial Hut. Just beyond a private gate, it swings through the wall. Bear left between the trees and boulders aproning the cliffs. Eventually meeting another path, turn up right through a breach to gain the ridge above Ⓐ.

Go left, shortly passing the quiet, mysterious-looking Doxey Pool on the right. Continue along the lofty ridge, eventually reaching a triangulation pillar marking its high point at 1,658 feet. Beyond, the way falls in a gradual descent, winding beside the weather worn formation of Bearstone Rock to meet a lane at Roach End Ⓑ. *It is at this point that the route can be shortened, crossing the road to a track that falls to the right beside a wall to a stile Ⓓ, just a little way down.*

Otherwise, cross the lane to a gap stile above the track. The onward path carries on through a gate to follow a wall along the continuing ridge. After a little less than ½ mile at a fork where both ways are signed to Dane Bridge, keep the higher path, which later drops to a shallow col. Ignore the crossing path and walk on through a narrow gate, eventually losing height to meet a sandy track **C**.

Signed to Gradbach, the way right falls across heather and bilberry heath, soon passing into Forest Wood. At a fork by a prominent outcrop of rock bear right to Lud's Church, looking for a path off a little farther along on the right. It slips through a narrow cleft in the sandstone cliff to descend into the deep moss and fern encrusted chasm of Lud's Church. Local tradition holds that this inaccessible spot was a meeting place for Lollards, a group of religious heretics prominent in the 14th and 15th centuries who followed John Wycliff. Persecution and the constant threat of execution by burning forced them to meet in secret hideouts, for which this place, supposedly named after one of the Lollards, Walter de Ludank would have been eminently suitable. Wind through and, as you begin to climb out at the far end, choose the right branch to find a stepped path to the top. Carry on among the trees, eventually passing a concessionary path (which leads back onto the ridge) to reach a T-junction just a short distance on. Turn right and, at a second junction go right again,

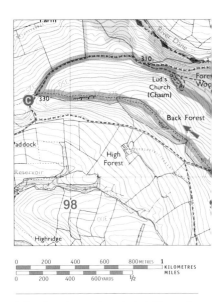

The Roaches

following signs to Roach End. The path breaks from the wood beside a wall at the edge of open heath, towards the top of which is a waymarked stile out onto a gravel track **D**.

Down the hill, beyond a farmhouse the way narrows to a path and continues along the flank into a quiet dale, eventually crossing a bridge over Black Brook. Bear right to a stile and carry on along the shallowing valley, later passing paths that lead off across Goldstitch Moss. Approaching Goldstitch House, negotiate a couple of stiles and keep forward across a track. Passing a barn, strike left towards a gate emerging onto a second track. Go right and bear left to a stone bridge. Cross and mount a stile beside a gate, and over a second stile a path begins skirting the rear of Blackbank Farm. Returning to the edge of the moor beyond, carry on above Black Brook once more. After crossing a stile and as the fence on the right then ends, curve left to accompany a rising ditch. Higher up, a wall corner forces you across the gully, the way continuing above its opposite bank to meet a lane.

Turn up the hill to a junction

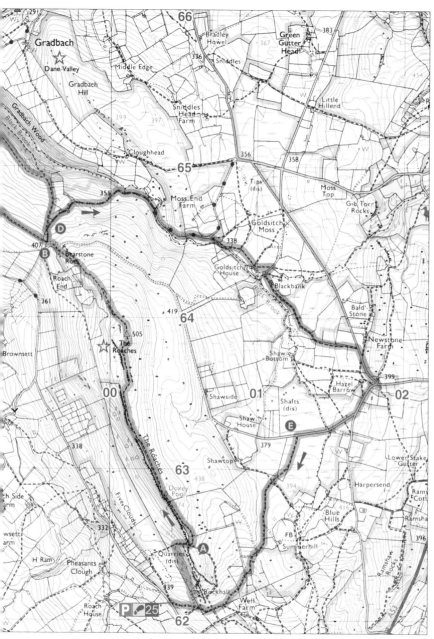

opposite Corner House and go right, bearing right again when you reach a fork. Carry on for a further ¼ mile then leave across a cattle-grid along a farm track on the left **E**. When it splits, keep with the right branch, which leads to the entrance of Summerhill Clough Farm. Abandon the track there through

a small gate on the right and follow a path beside a wall that climbs gently towards the top of the long ridge. Cresting the rise, the way then falls through the broad gap between The Roaches and Hen Cloud, finally returning you to the lane where you began the walk.

●

Eyam, Bretton Clough and Eyam Moor

		GPS waypoints
Start	Eyam	🖉 SK 216 767
Distance	9¼ miles (14.9km)	Ⓐ SK 211 765
Height gain	1,620 feet (494m)	Ⓑ SK 190 768
Approximate time	4½ hours	Ⓒ SK 190 779
Parking	Pay and Display opposite Eyam Museum	Ⓓ SK 200 779
		Ⓔ SK 210 794
Route terrain	Rough pasture and upland heath	Ⓕ SK 230 799
		Ⓖ SK 224 780
Ordnance Survey maps	Landranger 119 (Buxton & Matlock), Explorer OL24 (The Peak District – White Peak area)	Ⓗ SK 217 778
		Ⓙ SK 217 772
		Ⓚ SK 220 768

The plague village of Eyam is a fascinating place and lies amid outstandingly attractive countryside. The walk begins along field paths to Foolow, then climbs to Eyam Edge before dropping through the lovely, wooded valley of Bretton Clough. It continues along the valley of Highlow Brook, climbing back over the heathery expanses of Eyam Moor before returning to the village. This lengthy ramble embraces deep, wooded valleys, open moorland and magnificent views all the way, but perhaps its strongest appeal lies in the heroic story of Eyam itself during the plague years of 1665 and 1666.

In September 1665, when the Great Plague was at its height in London, George Viccars, a tailor lodging in the cottage of Mary Cooper in Eyam, died of a strange fever. He was the first of Eyam's plague victims and by the time it had run its course a year later, out of a population of around 350, over 260 lives had been lost, in some cases wiping out whole families. According to tradition, George Viccars was responsible for unwittingly introducing the disease into Eyam in an order of cloth from London. As the plague spread like wildfire through the small community, the villagers, under the courageous leadership of their vicars

Thomas Stanley and his successor William Mompesson, voluntarily cut themselves off from the outside world in order to stop the infection spreading. Food and medical supplies were left at various points on the village boundaries and the church was closed and services suspended, leaving families to bury their dead near their own homes. The village has many poignant reminders of those terrible events: the plague cottages by the church (where George Viccars lodged with Mary Cooper and the first death occurred), the numerous family graves scattered around, the Boundary Stone and Mompesson's Well on the edge of the village where

Eyam Moor

supplies were left to be collected. In the churchyard is the grave of Catherine Mompesson, the vicar's wife, who died on 25 August, 1666.

Leaving aside this single tragic event that had a profound effect on the village and made such a lasting impression on the rest of the country, Eyam is a most interesting and attractive place. Handsome stone cottages line its long main street and there is a fine, mainly 14th-century church with a Saxon font and a well-preserved Saxon cross in the churchyard. As well as the sad reminders of the plague, there is the unusual grave of the Derbyshire cricketer, Harry Bagshaw. It shows a wicket being hit by a ball and the raised finger of the umpire, indicating that his innings was over.

🖉 Turn left out of the car park opposite the museum and then right along the main street, passing the ruins of Bradshaw Hall on the right, which was once used as a cotton mill. Towards the top of the village, go sharp left into Tideswell Lane, climbing for some 250 yds to find a footpath leaving between houses on the right Ⓐ. Head away in an almost straight line across a succession of fields.

Although the landscape appears now largely pastoral, the area once rumbled to the sound of industry. Over to the right below the wooded slopes of Eyam Edge is Black Hole Mine, whilst on the left are the scars of Furness Quarry. After about $^3/_4$ mile, look out for a stile in the left-hand wall. The way strikes a shallow diagonal to dip through the depression of Linen Dale. Climbing out, continue forward at the edge of the subsequent fields until, at a gate stile approaching Foolow, a sign indicates a fork in the path. Strike right across the field to leave onto a lane, which then takes you into the village. A picturesque settlement, its stone cottages, pub and tiny church are grouped around the village pond and green where stands a medieval cross, erected there in 1868. Bear right, passing the **Bull's Head** and go right again at the next junction, following signs to Bretton Ⓑ.

Head away along the lane for almost $^1/_4$ mile, watching for a waymarked stile on the left, just beyond a track. Follow the right-hand wall away, continuing over a couple of stiles to the base of the Hucklow Edge escarpment. Climb through the cloaking bracken to a crossing track Ⓒ, which to the right returns you to Bradshaw Lane.

Carry on up the hill to the **Barrel Inn**, which has been a hostelry since at least the 17th century Ⓓ. Immediately before the pub, leave along a track on the left,

The Saxon cross in Eyam churchyard

following it for a little over ¼ mile. Where it bends right, just past a farm, walk ahead on a walled path behind cottages, continuing through a wicket gate and then a stile to the lip of a deep, wooded valley. The ongoing path zigzags steeply between the trees, crossing a stream at the bottom before winding through the more open heathland grazing beyond the foot of Bretton Clough. At a second broken wall where the trod splits, fork left below a ruined building. After dipping across a side stream, the way meanders along the main valley, eventually reaching a footbridge at Stoke Ford **E**.

Without crossing, carry on along the valley above Highlow Brook, shortly crossing another stream and then joining a track that gently loses height to a ford. Again remain on this bank, negotiating another side stream to mount a stile into a conifer plantation. Keep going in the fields beyond the trees, a track soon developing that leads to Tor Farm. Walk out along its access to a lane **F**.

Double back steeply up the hill, overlooking the Derwent Valley to Hathersage and the long line of a gritstone edge above the river. After almost ½ mile, leave at a waymarked gate and stile on the right, just opposite barns set below the lane. A clear path is signed to Sir William Hill Road, rising easily for nearly a mile over the sandy heather and bracken heath of Eyam Moor. It emerges at the far side onto the bend of a lane **G**.

Turn right onto a broad walled track, Sir William Hill Road, which was once part of a turnpike allegedly named after Sir William Cavendish, although several other local 'Sir Williams' could equally be candidates. Follow it up for almost ½ mile, looking for a signpost marking a crossing path, a little short of the top of the hill **H**. Go over the wall-stile on the left, following the field edge down towards Eyam.

Emerging onto a lane at the bottom **J** go left, but within a few yards, turn off through a small gate on the right. Strike diagonally to a wicket gate in the bottom corner and walk on to the top

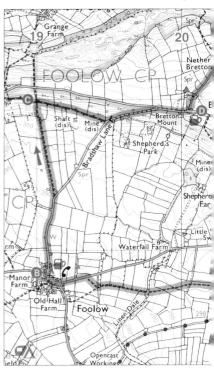

corner of a beech wood. Stay above the wood to another small gate at the far side of the field (not the one into the wood), beyond which a path falls across a steep wooded bank. Becoming paved lower down, it ends at a lane **K**.

Through a gate, opposite to the left, take the right-hand contained path downhill, continuing beside the left wall in the field below. Just right of the bottom corner, go over a stile and carry on down towards the back of the church. Walk through the graveyard to emerge on the main street and follow it right, past the plague cottages and the fine 17th-century façade of Eyam Hall before turning right to return to the car park. ●

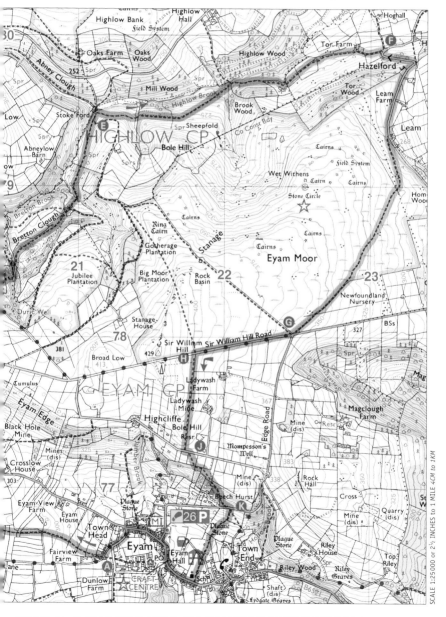

SCALE 1:25000 or 2½ INCHES to 1 MILE 4CM to 1KM

Bakewell, Chatsworth Park and the River Wye

		GPS waypoints	
Start	Bakewell		SK 219 684
Distance	10½ miles (16.9km) or 9¼ miles (14.9km) without detour to Haddon Hall	Ⓐ	SK 222 689
		Ⓑ	SK 235 697
		Ⓒ	SK 256 701
Height gain	1,290 feet (393m)	Ⓓ	SK 258 687
Approximate time	5 hours, shorter version 4½ hours	Ⓔ	SK 255 659
Parking	Smith's Island Pay and Display	Ⓕ	SK 244 669
Route terrain	Good tracks and clear field paths	Ⓖ	SK 229 670
Ordnance Survey maps	Landranger 119 (Buxton & Matlock), Explorer OL24 (The Peak District – White Peak area)		

In addition to its limestone dales, gritstone moors and lovely villages and towns, the Peak District is renowned for its great country houses, two of the finest being Chatsworth and Haddon, visited here. The walk also includes two particularly attractive stretches of riverside as well as woodland and meadows, and offers splendid views from the high ground between the Wye and Derwent valleys. It starts and finishes in the interesting old town of Bakewell.

Bakewell's intriguing blend of building styles spans the 16th to the present centuries, and reflects its varied and changing roles as an ancient market town, short-lived spa, textile producer and, more recently, an important tourist centre. Bakewell puddings, a well-known local delicacy, supposedly originated around 1860 as the result of an error made by a cook in one of the town's hotels. When asked to make a strawberry tart, he apparently put jam in first and poured the egg mixture over it, instead of the other way round.

🗒️ From the car park entrance, cross the river towards the town and then follow the riverbank up to the picturesque 14th-century stone bridge. Join the main road to re-cross the Wye,

turning right along Station Road and then left just beyond to climb Castle Hill. Approaching the former station at the top, leave along a lane on the right Ⓐ.

Cross the railway bridge to the old Station Master's House and then bear off onto a bridleway opposite. Keep ahead over a couple of golfers' paths and, after ringing the bell provided (to give warning of your presence), cross a fairway. Continue climbing through a bluebell wood, eventually emerging onto a lane at the top. Follow it right over the crest of the hill, beyond which, a magnificent view unfolds across the Derwent Valley to Chatsworth. After ½ mile, branch off right along an unsurfaced track Ⓑ.

In time it leads to the estate village of

Chatsworth House

Edensor, purpose-built by the sixth Duke of Devonshire between 1838 and 1842 to replace the original village, which spoiled his outlook across the park from Chatsworth House. Walk down through the village and bear left past the church to leave through gates onto the main road. Cross to a path opposite and follow it over the shoulder of a grassy hill. A magnificent view of Chatsworth suddenly appears ahead, a palatial mansion reached over an elegant 18th-century bridge and flanked by formal gardens against a glorious back-cloth of wooded hills. The present house, begun in 1686 for William Cavendish, the first Duke of Devonshire, befitted his prominent aristocracy. A tour includes the sumptuous state rooms, baroque chapel, painted hall, oak room (with superb wood carvings) and magnificent library. The early 19th century north wing includes an orangery, dining room, music gallery and sculpture gallery. The formal 17th-century gardens were extended by the Victorian architect and gardener Sir Joseph Paxton, who conceived the 280-foot Emperor Fountain, to honour an unrealised visit by the Russian Tsar. 'Capability' Brown laid out the extensive park, setting random groups of trees across the hillside and straightening the river. Removing Edensor to its present site completed the process, for neither man nor Nature was allowed to stand in the way of grand design.

From the bridge **Ⓒ**, it is only a short walk up the drive if you wish to visit the house. Otherwise, remain on this bank and cross the drive to follow a trod across the park. Cutting a bend of the river, aim for a clump of trees on a bluff overlooking the water. Carry on in the same direction, gaining height above the Derwent and eventually meeting the road by a cattle-grid **Ⓓ**.

Go left and then fork right along a lane past a car park and garden centre to Calton Lees, keeping with the lane as it later bends sharply left into the hamlet. Walk to the very end and climb a stile by a gate, from which a path follows the wall left to Rowsley. Cross a stile just before the corner into the adjacent field and head right to another stile beside a gate. Continue along the middle of successive fields, later meeting the river. As the field then begins to narrow, bear right and leave over a stile near the far end. Delve through a scrubby copse and carry on at the edge of another meadow to join a track. Keep going, eventually passing

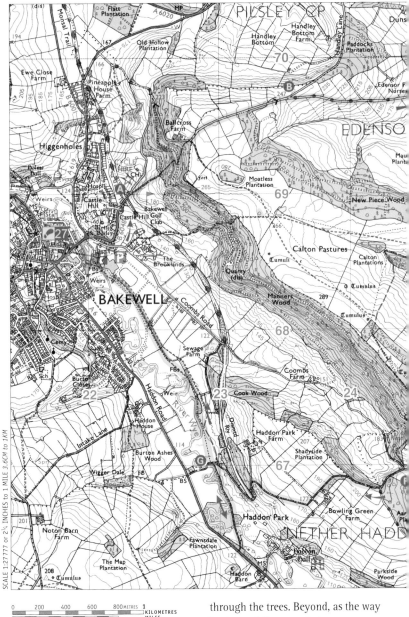

beneath a disused railway bridge and
emerging beside a farmyard onto a lane
at the edge of Rowsley **E**.

Turn right uphill past the church.
Beyond the last of the houses, the lane
narrows to a track, climbing between
fields and then at the edge of a
plantation. Passing a barrier, bear left

through the trees. Beyond, as the way
begins to fall, a grand view opens
across the Wye Valley. Remain with the
main track and continue down, passing
a second barrier to arrive at another
junction **F**. Again keep left, but then,
at a fork, go right, signed towards
Bakewell. After dropping past the
entrance to one of the Haddon Estate
farms, the track bends right. However,
leave it at that point to go forward on a

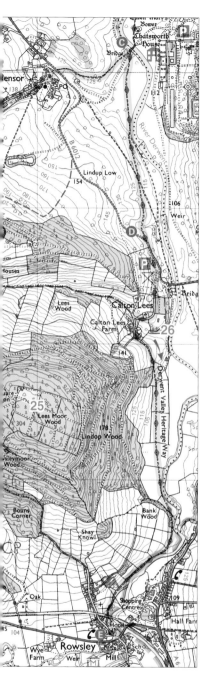

Approaching the river, look for a waymarked gate on the right **G**.

*There is now the option of a detour to Haddon Hall. In which case, continue past the gate to a stile on the left of the drive, from which a woodland path beside the river is signed to Haddon Hall. Later crossing the river, it rises to meet the main road. The entrance to the hall is then a short way to the left. Return to Point **G** to complete the last leg of the walk.*

The contrast between Chatsworth and Haddon is immediately obvious. The former is grand, formal and classical and set within a great sweep of landscaped parkland. Haddon, on the other hand, appears more the result of evolution than planning and has a series of intimate terraced gardens that rise above the river. It is essentially a late medieval manor house that came into the possession of the dukes of Rutland. Because it was not their main residence, they did little to modernise or extend it, which explains its largely unaltered appearance and unspoilt charm and authenticity. The main rooms are built around a paved courtyard, and particularly noteworthy are the panelled banqueting hall (complete with minstrels' gallery), medieval chapel and the marvellous light and airy long gallery, which has a beautifully decorated plaster ceiling.

From the waymarked gate **G**, follow a grass path, initially above the water meadows, but then soon dropping to hug the riverbank. Over a stile, pass through an area of wetland wood, crossing a footbridge into a field beyond. Keep going beside the hedge to shortcut the river's meanders, before long reaching the fields used for the Bakewell Show. Carry on ahead towards a large building, the Agricultural Business Centre, there turning left over a footbridge to return to Smith's Island. ●

bridlepath. Through a gate at the bottom, swing right and walk at the edge of successive fields to emerge onto a tarmac drive. Follow it left down the hill, curving sharply above the mouth of a tunnel, dug to take the railway through the hill beneath Haddon Hall.

Lathkill Dale

Start	Monyash		GPS waypoints
Distance	10½ miles (16.9km), shorter version 8½ miles (13.7km)		🖉 SK 149 666
			Ⓐ SK 172 653
Height gain	1,600 feet (488m)		Ⓑ SK 192 644
			Ⓒ SK 197 648
Approximate time	5 hours, shorter version 4 hours		Ⓓ SK 202 661
Parking	Car park in village		Ⓔ SK 212 656
Route terrain	Generally good, but occasionally rocky paths. *Note: the route through Lathkill Dale between Ⓓ and Ⓕ follows a permissive path, which is closed on Wednesdays between November and January*		Ⓕ SK 183 657
			Ⓖ SK 174 655
Ordnance Survey maps	Landranger 119 (Buxton & Matlock), Explorer OL24 (The Peak District – White Peak area)		

The Derbyshire Dales are famed for their outstanding beauty and, by any criteria, Lathkill Dale is one of the loveliest as this walk so richly demonstrates. Starting from the attractive village of Monyash, the route crosses open country, briefly dipping through the valley to Over Haddon. It soon meanders to the foot of the dale at Conksbury Bridge, from which there is a superlatively beautiful 3½ mile (5.6km) ramble along the steep sided, wooded banks of the Lathkill, undoubtedly the highlight of the walk. Emerging through a rocky gorge at the head of the dale, it is then only a short stroll back to Monyash.

Monyash, a farming and former lead-mining village, sits high on the limestone uplands near the head of Lathkill Dale. A fine 14th-century church and the base of a market cross on the village green hint at the settlement's importance during medieval times, when it grew as a market at the focus of routes through the region.

🖉 From the car park, go right to the crossroads and then left past the **village pub**. Turn into the churchyard and walk beside the church, leaving along a track beyond onto a lane. Follow it left to a bend and then keep ahead along a walled track, the Limestone Way. Take the left branch where it subsequently forks.

Through a gate at the end, accompany the right-hand wall to a second squeeze stile and then strike a left diagonal across the neighbouring field. Beyond a gap stile in the middle of the wall, keep with the Limestone Way beside the wall. Approaching the corner of the second field, slip through a gate and continue in the adjacent enclosure. Emerging at the bottom, join a track down to One Ash Grange Farm. As suggested by the name, this was once a monastic grange.

Keep ahead past the first barns but then, watch for a waymark directing

Along the Limestone Way

you left behind the main buildings and past a line of restored pigsties. A little farther along is a larder or dairy store, set below the cool of an overhanging limestone slab. At a fork bear right and pass between a large corrugated shed and old stone barns to a stile. *Be careful, for there is a deep drop into the field beyond.* Go forward along a shallow depression, passing through a gate into the head of Cales Dale. Descend a steep rocky path into the gorge, briefly levelling along a shelf beneath a limestone cliff before turning right to a stile and fingerpost at the bottom ⒜.

Climb a stepped path to the field above and head to a kissing-gate at the far side, glancing back for a superb view into upper Lathkill Dale. Maintain your direction across the next two pastures, and then go left to a kissing-gate into a wood. Walk straight through and cross a small paddock into more trees. In the field beyond, go right to a

gate and then strike a left diagonal to the far corner. Follow a path through the tip of Low Moor Plantation and keep the same line across the subsequent fields, a developing trod eventually guiding you to a gated stile, about halfway along the right-hand wall. Cross left to a second stile and walk the length of a final field, leaving onto a lane at the far corner ⒝.

Follow it left downhill for a little over ¼ mile before mounting a waymarked stile on the left ⒞. Bear right across the field, aiming for Over Haddon on the far hillside. Maintain the heading, eventually dropping towards a farm tucked into a fold. Skirt the corner of a wall as you approach, passing through a couple of gates into a large enclosure at the heart of the grange. Leave between the barns opposite to the field beyond, where a sign points half-right to Over Haddon. Through a gate in the corner, a track slopes steeply along the

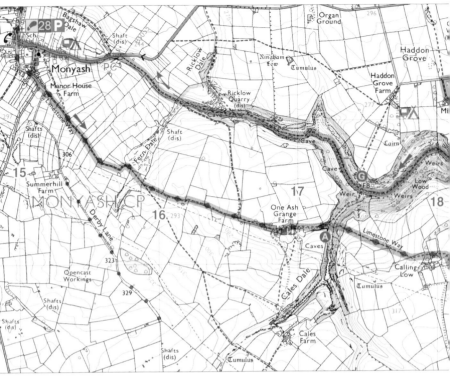

SCALE 1:26316 or 2½ INCHES to 1 MILE 3.8CM to 1KM

side of the Lathkill gorge, doubling back to a bridge across the river **D**.

You can shorten the walk at this point by omitting the loop through Over Haddon, in which case, a few paces up the lane ahead, turn off left along the valley path (See note opposite.)

However, the opportunity for refreshment in the village and fine panoramic views across the lower dale make the additional couple of miles well worth the effort. Carry on up the lane into the village, bearing right at a junction along the main street. Strung along the hillside at some 800 feet above sea level, this remote community enjoys striking vistas across Lathkill Dale and the valleys of the Wye and Derwent. Over Haddon's present tranquility belies its industrial past, for, like many other similarly sleepy Peakland villages, it was once a lead-mining settlement.

Where the road then bends left, keep ahead on School Lane, passing a Wesleyan chapel to go behind the **Lathkill Hotel**. As the lane doubles back on itself, leave over a gated squeeze stile in the corner and bear right across the slope of the field to another stile in the far wall. Keep the same angle across the next field to a gate in the lower fence and walk on along the lip of the gorge. Entering another field, wend right above the bottom wall. Where it later kinks down, look for a stile partly hidden by ivy and drop to a small parking area below. Follow the lane down to Conksbury Bridge, turning off right just before it onto a path beside the river **E**.

For the next 3½ miles, the walk winds beside the river through the exceptionally beautiful Lathkill Dale. The character of the valley is constantly

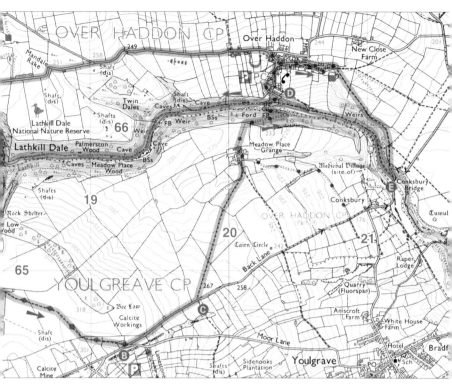

changing, from lush woodland rich in wild flowers and harbouring many small birds at this end to a Spartan rocky gorge at the other. The river is crystal clear and supports a wide range of plants, insects and fish, and the water birds that feed upon them. Prolonged good weather can make the river disappear, although the water still flows deep underground, seeping through a maze of natural caves and old mine workings. Reaching Lathkill Lodge, where you first crossed the river **D**, turn up the lane as before, but almost immediately, leave through a gate to continue on a permissive riverside path.

*Note: should the path be closed, the detour from Point **D** is via Over Haddon and along the lane west. Keep ahead at a fork and continue for a further ½ mile before turning in at the entrance to Mill Farm. Walk between the buildings and out along a walled track that winds down a side dale to return to Lathkill*

*Dale at Point **F**.*

A little farther along, a bridge provides access to the remains of Bateman's House; a miner's dwelling built on top of the shaft. Bring a torch for a ladder gives access to a chamber beneath, where a pump was installed to lift water from the mine. Return to the path and carry on up the valley, later emerging briefly from the woods to cross a small meadow at the mouth of a side dale. Notice a couple of discarded millstones beside the path just beyond there. Keep going, eventually passing a bridge across the river at the foot of Cales Dale **G**.

As you progress, the gorge narrows and before long, there is no water flowing over the bouldery streambed. Beyond the debris of a redundant quarry, the gorge opens to the head of the dale. Carry on along a slight grassy fold through a couple of fields, finally emerging onto a lane. Follow it left back into Monyash.

Further Information

Safety on the Hills

The hills, mountains and moorlands of Britain, though of modest height compared with those in many other countries, need to be treated with respect. Friendly and inviting in good weather, they can quickly be transformed into wet, misty, windswept and potentially dangerous areas of wilderness in bad weather. Even on an outwardly fine and settled summer day, conditions can rapidly deteriorate at high altitudes and, in winter, even more so.

Therefore it is advisable to always take both warm and waterproof clothing, sufficient nourishing food, a hot drink, first-aid kit, torch and whistle. Wear suitable footwear, such as strong walking-boots or shoes that give a good grip over rocky terrain and on slippery slopes. Try to obtain a local weather forecast and bear it in mind before you start. Do not be afraid to abandon your proposed route and return to your starting point in the event of a sudden and unexpected deterioration in the weather. Do not go alone and allow enough time to finish the walk well before nightfall.

Most of the walks described in this book do not venture into remote wilderness areas and will be safe to do, given due care and respect, at any time of year in all but the most unreasonable weather. Indeed, a crisp, fine winter day often provides perfect walking conditions, with firm ground underfoot and a clarity that is not possible to achieve in the other seasons of the year. A few walks, however, are suitable only for reasonably fit and experienced hill walkers able to use a compass and should definitely not be tackled by anyone else during the winter months or in bad weather, especially high winds and mist. These are indicated in the general description that precedes each of the walks.

Walkers and the Law

The Countryside and Rights of Way Act (CRoW Act 2000) extends the rights of access previously enjoyed by walkers in England and Wales. Implementation of these rights began on 19 September 2004. The Act amends existing legislation and for the first time provides access on foot to certain types of land – defined as mountain, moor, heath, down and registered common land.

Where You Can Go
Rights of Way
Prior to the introduction of the CRoW Act, walkers could only legally access the countryside along public rights of way. These are either 'footpaths' (for walkers only) or 'bridleways' (for walkers, riders on horseback and pedal cyclists). A third category called 'Byways open to all traffic' (BOATs), is used by motorised vehicles as well as those using non-mechanised transport. Mainly they are green lanes, farm and estate roads, although occasionally they will be found crossing mountainous area.

Rights of way are marked on Ordnance Survey maps. Look for the green broken lines on the Explorer maps, or the red dashed lines on Landranger maps.

The term 'right of way' means exactly what it says. It gives a right of passage over what, for the most part, is private land. Under pre-CRoW legislation walkers were required to keep to the line of the right of way and not stray onto land on either side. If you did inadvertently wander off the right of way, either because of faulty map reading or because the route was not clearly indicated on the ground, you were technically trespassing.

Local authorities have a legal obligation to ensure that rights of way are kept clear and free of obstruction, and are signposted where they leave metalled roads. The duty of local authorities to install signposts extends to the placing of signs along a path or way, but only where the authority considers it necessary to have a signpost or waymark to assist persons unfamiliar with the locality.

THE
FESTIVE FOOD
OF
FRANCE

Marie-Pierre Moine

ILLUSTRATED BY SALLY MALTBY

SERIES EDITOR: HENRIETTA GREEN

KYLE CATHIE LIMITED

Dedication
For Michèle Richet with thanks and affection

First published 1991 by
Kyle Cathie Limited
20 Vauxhall Bridge Road, London SW1V 2SA

Reprinted 1995

ISBN 1 85626 200 6

A CIP catalogue record for this book is available
from the British Library

Designed and typeset by Geoff Hayes
on his posh new AppleMac

Printed and bound by Chromo Litho, Italy

Contents

La Fête des Rois

TWELFTH NIGHT

On January 6th children all over France go to school in happy anticipation of the final treat of the Christmas celebrations – *la Galette des Rois.* If they are lucky, children will eat it twice, at lunchtime in the school canteen and again at home in the evening.

What makes the almond puff pastry cake particularly exciting is that it conceals a small bean-like china token, a *fève,* which one lucky person will find in his wedge of *galette* (making a great show of nearly breaking a tooth or choking), and which makes him or her king or queen for the evening, complete with golden cardboard crown. Most people nowadays buy their *galette* from the local *pâtisserie,* but it always comes complete with token and crown.

Twelfth Night commemorates the visit of the three kings to the crib and marks the end of the Christmas festivities, but the idea of the lucky king of the feast goes back to wild rites and pre-Christian times, when the 'feast' the 'king' presided over tended to be a drunken and often bloody orgy – a far cry from the quiet family celebration it has become in France.

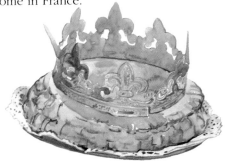

Galette des Rois
(TWELFTH NIGHT CAKE)

serves 6
300g/10½oz puff pastry
egg yolk and 1tablespoon/1½tablespoons milk
  for glazing

Filling
170g/6oz/1½cups ground almonds
grated zest of 1 small orange
20ml/1tablespoon/1½tablespoons kirsch
100g/3½oz/½cup caster sugar
100g/3½oz/½cup unsalted butter, softened
small token (or ceramic bean)

1 Divide the puff pastry into two pieces and roll
out each piece into a circle, about 20–25cm/8–10in
in diameter. Line a baking sheet with greaseproof
paper and place one circle of pastry in the centre.
2 To prepare the filling, combine the ground
almonds, orange zest, kirsch, caster sugar and
butter until smooth.
3 Spread the filling evenly over the circle of
pastry, leaving a 2.5cm/1in border. Tuck the token
into the filling, somewhere halfway between the
centre and the edge.
4 Using a pastry brush, moisten the border of the
circle with a little glazing mixture. Carefully
position the second circle of puff pastry over the
first, pressing gently around the edge to seal it.
Prick the pastry in several places with a fork. Using
a sharp knife, cut a criss-cross pattern all over.
Brush the whole surface lightly with the rest of the
glazing mixture.
5 Bake for 20–30 minutes in a preheated 200°C/
400°F/gas6 oven until golden and puffed, taking
care not to open the oven door during the first 15
minutes. Serve warm.

La Fête des Omelettes

OMELETTE FEAST

Every year on February 10th after a long absence of nearly one hundred days the sun makes a welcome return to the tiny mountain village of Les Andrieux in the Hautes-Alpes of northern Provence. The inhabitants traditionally celebrate this long-awaited reappearance by making omelettes.

Omelette traditionnelle

(TRADITIONAL FRENCH OMELETTE)

serves 2

4 large eggs
20ml/1tablespoon/1½tablespoons water
30g/1oz butter
salt and freshly ground black pepper

1 Lightly beat the eggs with the water. Season to taste with salt and freshly ground black pepper.
2 Heat a small, heavy-based frying-pan. Add most of the butter to the hot pan, reserving a knob to finish the omelette. When the butter is very hot but not burning, pour in the egg mixture. Leave to settle for a moment, then start slowly stirring up the mixture towards the centre. As soon as the eggs begin to look just set but still moist, fold one quarter of the omelette towards the centre, then fold over the opposite side. Cook for a moment longer, then invert the omelette on a warmed serving plate. Trail the remaining butter over it and serve immediately.

Fillings for two 4-egg omelettes

Provençal vegetable
30ml/1½ tablespoons/2tablespoons olive oil
1 small red pepper, cored, deseeded and thinly
    sliced
1 small bulb fennel, halved, trimmed and sliced
    into thin segments
2 spring onions, finely chopped
½ garlic clove, finely chopped
sprig of fresh thyme or pinch of dried
salt and freshly ground black pepper

1 Heat the oil in a pan over a medium-high heat,
then add the prepared vegetables and the thyme.
Cook for about 10–15 minutes, stirring frequently
until the vegetables are soft and golden brown.
Season to taste.
2 Cook the omelettes and just before folding
spoon half the vegetables on the centre of each.

Jam
100ml/4fl oz/½cup apricot or raspberry jam, or
    redcurrant jelly
10ml/2teaspoons brandy, *eau de vie* or liqueur
10ml/2teaspoons caster sugar for the omelettes
icing sugar for dredging

1 Combine the jam or jelly with the brandy or
liqueur.
2 Prepare the omelette as described opposite, but
adding the caster sugar and using only the tiniest
pinch of salt. Cook and fill as described, and dredge
with icing sugar just before serving.

Le Carnaval

CARNIVAL

The annual Carnival, preceding the forty lean days of Lent has always been celebrated with feasting and merry-making, and colourful parades and processions of floats and, in the north, gigantic mannequins.

In Paris the doomed star of Carnival was traditionally a huge ox, *le Bœuf Gras*. This carefully selected specimen could weigh over 1800 kilos/ 4000 pounds and its meat went to the master-butchers. Apprentices also had 'their' share of the beast. This they used to tie to a piece of string labelled with their name and cook in a vast communal pot. The young butchers' Carnival dish, *Bœuf Ficelle*, has remained one of the classics of French cooking.

Bœuf Ficelle

(BEEF POACHED IN STOCK)

serves 4

700g/1⅔lb piece of lean fillet or rumpsteak
1.1 litres/2pints/5cups light veal or beef stock
450g/1lb carrots, peeled and chopped
450g/1lb baby turnips, peeled and chopped
225g/8oz brown cap mushrooms, wiped and sliced
20ml/1tablespoon/1½tablespoons brandy
30g/1oz butter
40ml/2tablespoons/3tablespoons finely chopped
   flat-leaf parsley
coarse sea salt
black pepper
Dijon mustard

1 Bring the stock to the boil in a large saucepan. Add the carrots and turnips, reduce the heat and simmer for 10–12 minutes, then add the mushrooms and sprinkle with the brandy and continue simmering for 2–3 minutes.

2 Meanwhile, tie the beef securely with a piece of string long enough for you to hang it from the handle or handles of the pan during cooking.

3 Remove the vegetables from the pan with a slotted spoon and keep warm.

4 Bring the stock to the boil and carefully plunge the beef into the boiling liquid. Tie the string to the handles – the meat should not touch the bottom of the pan. Return to the boil, then simmer for about 20–25 minutes, depending on how well done you like your beef. If the piece of beef is long rather than chunky, it will cook faster, about 15–20 minutes.

5 Remove the beef from the stock and place on a warmed dish. Return the vegetables to the stock to reheat briefly. Discard the string and cut the beef into 4 slices. Dot with butter and sprinkle with parsley. Arrange the vegetables around the meat and moisten them with a little stock. Serve with coarse sea salt, black pepper and mustard. Save the rest of the stock for another recipe.

Mardi Gras

SHROVE TUESDAY

'If you want your wheat to stay free of black rot, you must eat pancakes on Shrove Tuesday.' Cooking and eating pancakes or fritters on the last day of Carnival was believed to bring you luck and to this day the family frying-pan is put to good use all over France on the evening of Mardi Gras.

Fritters come in many guises: flower blossoms in Provence where spring comes early, apples in Normandy, curd cheese in the centre are just three.

Mardi Gras pancakes are wafer-thin and sweet. They are served with butter, sugar and a dash of lemon, or more traditionally with soft brown sugar (*cassonade*), and thick cream.

Pâte à Crêpes Bretonne
(BRITTANY PANCAKES)

makes about 18

250g/8½oz/2cups flour
pinch of salt
1 large egg, lightly beaten
100g/3½oz/½cup
  caster sugar

milk
30g/1oz butter, melted
20ml/1tablespoon/
  1½tablespoons rum

1 Sift the flour and salt into a bowl. Work in the egg and sugar, then stir in enough milk to make a light, creamy batter. Stir in the melted butter and rum, and leave to rest for at least 20 minutes.
2 Just before cooking, stir a little extra milk or water into the batter if it looks too thick. Lightly grease a 12.5–15cm/5–6in pan, place it over a medium heat until hot, then spoon in 2–3 tablespoons batter. Swirl and cook for just over 1 minute on each side.

Beignets aux Pommes et au Cidre
(APPLE AND CIDER FRITTERS)

serves 6

250g/8½oz/2cups
  self-raising flour
pinch of salt
275g/9½oz/1⅙cups
  caster sugar, plus
  extra for sprinkling
finely grated zest of 1
  small lemon
100ml/4fl oz/½cup water
150ml/¼pint/⅔cup milk
20ml/1tablespoon/
  1½tablespoons sunflower
  or groundnut oil

250ml/⅓pint/1cup
  dry cider
550g/1¼lb eating apples
100ml/4fl oz/½cup
  Calvados or
  apple brandy
oil for deep-fat frying
cream, to serve

1 Sift the flour, salt, sugar (reserving 55g/2oz/
¼cup) and lemon zest into a large bowl, then
make a well in the centre. Combine the water,
milk, oil and cider and pour this liquid, a little at a
time, into the centre of the well. Stir in the dry
ingredients until you have a smooth batter. Cover
and leave to rest for 30 minutes.

2 Meanwhile, peel and core the apples, then cut
them into thick rings. Combine the rest of the sugar
with the Calvados or brandy and coat the apple
rings with the mixture.

3 Heat the oil in a deep frying-pan or deep-fat
fryer over a medium-high heat. When hot (about
180°C/350°F) dip the apple rings a few at a time in
the batter and fry them for about 3 minutes until
crisp and golden all over.

4 Drain well on absorbent paper. Sprinkle with a
little sugar and serve hot, with a jug of cream.

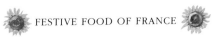

Foire au Boudin

BLACK PUDDING FAIR

The third weekend in March, the Black Pudding
Fair, is the highlight of the year in the Normandy
town of Mortagne-au-Perche. Hundreds of
competitors from France and abroad enter their
black puddings in the annual championship – by
express post or in person – while people with
hearty appetites prepare themselves to wolf down
large quantities of the stuff in order to win the
coveted title of champion *boudin* eater …

There are as many types of *boudin* as there are butchers making it but it tends to be a spicy mixture of pig's blood and fat encased in gut and then poached. It is traditionally served pan-fried with fried apple slices and/or creamed potatoes.

Boudin Poêlé Sauce Moutarde

(PAN-FRIED BLACK PUDDING WITH MUSTARD SAUCE)
serves 2

200g/7oz French-style *boudin* or English black pudding
10ml/2teaspoons oil
30g/1oz butter
50ml/3tablespoons/¼cup dry white wine
20ml/1tablespoon/1½tablespoons thick cream
10ml/2teaspoons Dijon mustard
salt and freshly ground black pepper

1 If using *boudin*, cut it across into 2 pieces and prick several times with a fork. If using thicker black pudding, cut it into 2.5cm/1in slices, then remove the skin.

2 In a large frying-pan heat the oil and half the butter over a moderate heat. Reduce the heat and add the *boudin* or black pudding. Sauté gently. If using *boudin* cook for 12–15 minutes, turning the sausages over to cook them evenly. If using black pudding, cook for 5 minutes on each side. In either case keep the heat low to prevent the sausage disintegrating. Remove from the pan and keep warm.

3 Turn up the heat. Add the wine to the pan and stir with the pan juices until slightly reduced. Stir in the cream and mustard. Heat through, turn off the heat and whisk in the rest of the butter. Season lightly with salt and more generously with pepper. Spoon the sauce over the black pudding and serve immediately.

Vendredi Saint

GOOD FRIDAY

The most significant Friday of the year is Good Friday when the traditional Lenten dish *Brandade de Morue*, a pounded salt cod concoction, is served all over France.

As a predominantly Catholic country, France used to obey the Church's fasting rules very strictly. No meat was ever to be consumed on Fridays or during Lent and, if you wanted to eat butter on such 'lean' days, you had to give the church a special offering, which proved to be an excellent source of income.

Creamily fishy, *Brandade* is just the thing for eating on Good Friday: it keeps well and, served with potatoes and followed by a salad, is substantial enough to sustain people through the lengthy services and rigours of the day.

For the last two centuries salt cod, originally from Provence, has been easily available throughout France. It may be an acquired taste but devotees go to great lengths to indulge themselves. Monsieur Thiers, a nineteenth-century gourmand, statesman and briefly President of the Republic, was forbidden *Brandade* by his doctors. Undaunted and determined not to be deprived, he persuaded a fellow enthusiast to smuggle the dish into his office, hidden under official documents.

18

Brandade de Morue
(SALT COD PROVENÇALE)

serves 4

450g/1lb salt cod
bouquet garni
200ml/7fl oz olive oil
100ml/4fl oz/½cup milk
2–3 garlic cloves,
  finely chopped
75ml/5tablespoons/⅓cup
  thick cream

juice of 1 lemon
freshly ground black
  pepper, to taste
freshly grated nutmeg,
  to taste

1 Soak the salt cod overnight, preferably up to
12–14 hours, in plenty of cold water, changing the
water several times to get rid of the saltiness.
2 Break the fish into chunks. Place in a large
saucepan with the bouquet garni, cover with fresh
cold water and bring to the boil. Reduce the heat
and simmer very gently for 10–15 minutes without
letting it boil as this would toughen the flesh.
3 Remove the flesh from the pan, drain it well and
discard the skin and as many bones as possible.
Then, in a large bowl, shred or mash the fish into
small pieces.
4 Meanwhile, gently heat the olive oil and milk in
separate pans. Pour half the warm olive oil over
the fish and pound vigorously, using a large pestle
or wooden spoon.
5 Work in the garlic, the remaining oil and the
milk, a little at a time until you end up with a thick
purée. This will probably take around 10 minutes.
6 Stir in the cream and lemon juice and season
  with the pepper and nutmeg. Return the mixture to
  a pan, add the butter and reheat gently. Serve with
  garlic croûtons.

La Foire aux Jambons

HAM FAIR

Everywhere in France the end of Lent has always
meant indulging once more in dishes that are
forbidden during lean days. What can be less lean
than a rotund pig? The most celebrated ham fair,
La Foire aux Jambons, used to take place in Paris
around the time of Holy Week. It still takes place
but has moved from its grand setting in front of
Notre Dame to the more modest suburb of Chatou.

One of the most delectable of the ham dishes
originated in Burgundy. *Jambon Persillé*, cubes of
ham set in a white wine jelly, has become the
specialité de la maison of many a *charcuterie* of
the region. At Easter it is served in a round white
china bowl, sometimes with hardboiled eggs set
inside the hams, a seasonal touch. Festive cooking is
not for people with small appetites, particularly in
Burgundy, where *Jambon Persillé* tends to be eaten
as a starter, with pickled gherkins and bread. It is
substantial enough to make a satisfying and
attractive main course, served with a salad.

Jambon Persillé

(JELLIED HAM WITH PARSLEY)

serves 8

1.5kg/3½lb piece of gammon or ham, rinsed
beef marrow bone or veal knuckle, chopped in half
2 calves' feet, split
1 Spanish onion studded with 4 cloves
2 each of shallots and carrots
bouquet garni
a few sprigs of chervil and tarragon

pinch each of dried marjoram and tarragon
8 black peppercorns
700ml/1¼pints/3cups dry white wine
200g/7oz finely chopped flat-leaf parsley
20ml/1tablespoon/1½tablespoons white wine
    vinegar
freshly ground black pepper

1 Rinse the gammon or ham. Put it in a large
saucepan, cover with water and bring to the boil
over a moderate heat. Simmer for 30 minutes.
2 Remove the meat from the pan. Discard the
cooking liquid and rinse out the pan. Divide the
meat into 4 pieces. Cut out and discard any rind or
excessively fatty bits.
3 Return the meat to the pan, with the beef
marrow or veal knuckle, the calves' feet, onion,
shallots, carrots, bouquet garni, herbs and peppercorns. Pour in the wine. Bring to the boil over a low
heat, cover and simmer very gently for 2 hours,
skimming off any fat from time to time.
4 Leave to cool, remove the meat with a slotted
spoon and put into a large bowl. Strain the
cooking liquid through a sieve and keep warm.
5 Using two forks, lightly flake the meat. Stir in 2
tablespoons of the parsley and the vinegar. Season
to taste with freshly ground black pepper.
6 In a wetted salad bowl or a 1.1litre/2pint/5cup
loaf tin, sprinkle a layer of chopped parsley, then
spread a layer of flaked meat over, and continue
alternating, ending up with a thick layer of parsley.
7 Trickle the cooking liquid into the dish, allowing
it to seep under the parsley. Cover, place a weight
on top and set overnight in the refrigerator.
8 Serve in the bowl or turned out. To turn out the
jellied ham, soak a tea towel in hot water, wring it
out and wrap it around the base of the bowl or tin
for a minute. Invert onto a plate. The jellied ham
will keep for several days in the refrigerator.

Pâques

EASTER

On Easter morning, when church bells are ringing out all over the country, French children are busy looking for Easter eggs hidden around the garden or house before the traditional family lunch. The symbol of new life, eggs have always been at the heart of Easter celebrations, and eggs laid on Good Friday were thought to have magic properties. In our commercial era Easter eggs tend to come in shop-bought chocolate form, but for centuries they were plainly hardboiled. Children and youths begged for eggs from door to door and played ritual games with them. They were rolled down long planks, rather like *boules*, and the winner's egg was the one that remained intact. The eggs were then chopped into salads or pies. In the south-east tinted hardboiled eggs are still embedded in ring-shaped sweet cakes which children wear as edible armlets.

For many French families an Easter feast would be incomplete without an expensive *gigot pascal*, a roast leg of lamb. Dried haricot beans simmered until tender are a traditional accompaniment in the west of the country. In the north-east where fewer sheep are raised, the great Easter symbol is a lamb-shaped cake rather than an actual roast...

Œufs en Chocolat
(CHOCOLATE EGGS)

makes 6

6 small or medium eggs (plus a few spares in case of accidents)

500g/1lb/2oz dark, milk or white chocolate (or a combination of the three), plus extra for decoration (optional)

candied angelica leaves for decoration (optional)

1 Holding an egg very carefully in one hand, delicately pierce a small hole at both ends with a needle. Gently blow out the contents of the egg (you may find it helpful to insert a short straw into one end and blow into the straw). Carefully enlarge one hole until it is about 5mm/¼in wide. Wash the egg under running cold water and leave to drain. Repeat the operation with the remaining eggs.

2 Once the shells are completely dry stick a small piece of foil over each of the small holes (using sticky tape rather than glue).

3 Break the chocolate into a small bowl (use as many bowls as you have types of chocolate). Place the bowl over a saucepan of simmering water and melt the chocolate, stirring occasionally.

4 Once the chocolate has completely melted, carefully spoon it into the egg shells through the larger holes, making sure that there are no air bubbles. If you prefer, slowly trickle the chocolate into the shells with the help of a small funnel. Refrigerate the eggs for a few hours until set.

5 Gently crack the shells and remove to reveal the chocolate eggs. If you like, decorate the eggs with trimmed angelica leaves by sticking them to the eggs with a little melted chocolate.

Gigot aux Flageolets
(LEG OF LAMB WITH HARICOT BEANS)

serves 6

1 part-boned leg of new-season lamb, trimmed
    French style, weighing about 1.8kg/4lb
900g/2lb dried flageolet or white haricot beans,
    soaked overnight
3 large Spanish onions, peeled
5 garlic cloves
bouquet garni
a few springs of thyme
2 bay leaves
85g/3oz/⅓cup butter
5 shallots
2 ripe tomatoes, skinned, deseeded and chopped
100ml/4fl oz/½cup dry white wine
salt and freshly ground black pepper

1 Bring to the boil a large saucepan of cold water
with the soaked beans. Drain well, return to the
pan, cover with boiling water and add 2 onions, 1
garlic clove, the bouquet garni, sprigs of thyme and
bay leaves. Bring back to the boil and simmer for
at least 1½ hours, seasoning with salt and pepper
after 1 hour. The beans should be just soft but not
collapsing. Test occasionally, because the exact
timing depends on the beans you use. Drain.
2 Meanwhile, bring the leg of lamb to room
temperature. Heat the oven and a roasting tin to
230°C/450°F/gas8. Cut the rest of the garlic cloves
into slivers. Using a small sharp knife, make small
cuts in the meat and push in the garlic slivers. Dot
with 30g/1oz butter and season liberally with salt
and pepper. Roast the lamb, allowing 12–16
minutes for each 450g/1lb, depending on how pink
you like your lamb to be.
3 Prepare a sauce. Finely chop the last onion and
the shallots. Melt the rest of the butter in a small
saucepan, and sweat the prepared onion and

shallots gently without letting them brown. Add the prepared tomatoes and cook slowly until soft, then add half the wine, season lightly and continue cooking for a few minutes.

4 Once the lamb is cooked, pour half its cooking juices into the sauce mixture. Spread the beans in a large gratin dish. Pour the sauce mixture over the beans and stir gently until they are well soaked. Put the lamb on top of the beans and place the dish in the oven. Turn off the heat after 5 minutes and leave to stand in the hot oven for a further 10 minutes.

5 While the dish is settling in the oven, pour the rest of the wine into the roasting tin, stir with the remaining cooking juices over a brisk heat, then strain into a sauceboat and serve with the lamb.

Salade aux Pissenlits
(DANDELION SALAD)

serves 6

250g/8½oz dandelion leaves, trimmed, rinsed and drained
100g/3½oz lettuce leaves, trimmed, rinsed and drained
20ml/1tablespoon/1½tablespoons white or red wine vinegar
75ml/5tablespoons/⅓cup light olive oil
garlic croûtons
1 hardboiled egg, chopped
6 black olives, stoned and chopped
salt and freshly ground black pepper

1 Combine the vinegar and oil and season with salt and pepper to taste.

2 Pour this dressing over the salad leaves and toss until well coated. Sprinkle in the croûtons, chopped hardboiled egg and olives. Toss again lightly, check seasoning and serve.

Saint Honoré

The namedays of saints feature prominently on the colourful calendar issued by the post office which has become a national institution to be seen hanging in most French kitchens. It is a reminder that every craft and profession traditionally has its own patron; May 16th is the Feast of Saint-Honoré, patron saint of bakers, traditionally portrayed holding the long-handled oven peel, or shovel, of his trade.

This elaborate choux paste and cream concoction is named after him.

Gâteau Saint Honoré

(ST HONORE'S CAKE)

serves 6–8
225g/8oz shortcrust
  pastry
1tablespoon
  1½tablespoons
  caster sugar
10ml/2teaspoons
  ground almonds

Choux paste
150ml/¼pint/⅔cup water
55g/2oz/¼cup butter, diced
pinch of salt
75g/2½oz/¾cup flour
2 large eggs, beaten
few drops of
  vanilla essence

Glaze
1 small egg and a little milk, beaten

Crème Chantilly
400ml/⅔pint/1¾cups
  double cream
icing sugar to taste
20ml/1 tablespoon/
  1½tablespoons
  iced water
10ml/2 teaspoons
  kirsch

Caramel Syrup
100g/3½oz/½cup
  caster sugar
50ml/3tablespoons/
  ¼cup water

1 Roll out the shortcrust pastry into a thin 20cm/ 8in circle. Sprinkle it with the sugar and ground almonds, pressing in lightly. Spread the circle on a greased baking sheet and chill for 20 minutes.

2 To make the choux paste, bring the water, diced butter and salt to the boil in a heavy-based saucepan. Remove the boiling liquid from the heat and quickly stir in the flour with a wooden spoon. Return to a medium-hot heat and stir briskly until the paste is shiny and comes off the sides of the pan. Beat in the eggs until the paste is glossy. Flavour with a few drops of vanilla essence.

3 Fit a piping bag with a plain 1cm/½in nozzle and pipe a ring of paste around the chilled pastry circle 5mm/¼in from the edge.

4 Use the rest of the choux paste to pipe small puffs onto a second greased baking sheet, keeping them well apart. Brush the choux paste circle and puffs lightly with glaze.

5 Bake the ring and the small puffs for 10 minutes in a preheated 220°C/425°F/gas7 oven, then open the oven door for a minute, turn down the heat to 190°C/375°F/gas5 and bake for a further 10–15 minutes until firm and dry. Leave to cool on a rack.

6 Make the Crème Chantilly. Whisk the cream. Sift in icing sugar to taste, then beat until stiff. Fold in the iced water and kirsch. Slit open the puffs and spoon in a little Crème Chantilly. Chill the choux and the rest of the cream until needed. Prepare the caramel syrup. In a small saucepan heat the sugar in the water until the sugar has dissolved, stirring constantly. Boil until the syrup thickens and turns a pale gold. Remove from the heat. Using tongs, quickly and carefully dip the choux puffs into the syrup, then arrange them on top of the choux paste ring. Spoon the rest of the Crème Chantilly into the centre of the cake and serve as soon as possible, or keep chilled until needed.

Foires aux Asperges

ASPARAGUS FAIRS

Wherever asparagus happens to be the pride of the local produce, the start of the new season is a happy occasion. Many villages hold an asparagus fair, where growers proudly display the best of their crop to a gallery of critical experts. For the French, asparagus is the most highly prized of vegetables. Everybody has strong views about the precious stalks – which variety tastes best, how to accommodate it and whether to serve it hot, warm or cold. In the Sologne area of the Loire where it was introduced by a retired policeman just over a century ago, asparagus even have their own fan club, La Confrérie des Mangeux d'Esparges, the brotherhood of asparagus-eaters. Twice a year members put on purple robes trimmed with white and solemnly meet to enjoy a good meal and talk about *asperges*.

Asperges au Naturel
(PLAIN-COOKED ASPARAGUS)

serves 4

550g/1¼lb asparagus   salt

1 Trim the asparagus of woody ends and tough fibrous skin if necessary. Rinse well. Tie the stalks in bundles and stand the bundles in glass jars. Fill with boiling salted water to just below the tips, cover with foil and place in a large, deep pan of simmering water. Cook until the asparagus feel just tender when pierced with a knife below the tips. This will take 10–35 minutes, depending on the asparagus.

2 Drain well on a clean thick tea towel and serve warm, with lemon butter or anchovy vinaigrette.

Beurre Citronné
(LEMON BUTTER)
40ml/2tablespoons/3tablespoons water
100g/3½oz/½cup butter
juice of ½ small lemon
salt and white pepper

Bring the water to the boil in a small saucepan.
Remove from the heat, swirl in the butter until
melted and season to taste with a little salt, pepper
and lemon juice.

Vinaigrette à l'Anchois
(ANCHOVY VINAIGRETTE)
100ml/4fl oz/½cup light olive oil
40ml/2tablespoons/3tablespoons red wine vinegar
1–2 anchovy fillets, drained of oil and mashed, or
   1teaspoon anchovy essence
freshly ground black pepper
a few sprigs each of flat-leaf parsley, chives,
   tarragon and/or chervil

Whisk together the olive oil, vinegar, mashed
anchovy fillets or anchovy essence. Season to taste
with pepper. Snip the fresh herbs and stir them
into the vinaigrette.

Le Temps des Cerises

THE CHERRY SEASON

Quand reviendra le temps des cerises... when it is cherry time again, according to the song, people's thoughts turn to romance and jollity. Villages everywhere make merry at cherry festivals and *Clafoutis* (from the French patois, *clafir*, to garnish) takes pride of place in the front windows of the *pâtisseries*. This cherry custard pudding is one of the most traditional of France's fruit desserts. The stones are normally left in the cherries, which does great things for the flavour of the pudding but may be hazardous for young children and people unfamiliar with this dish.

In some regions it is baked on top of a large buttered cabbage leaf – but it does taste just as good cooked in a more conventional container! When the cherry season is over, this favourite French dessert is worth making with plums (stoned and halved) or apples (cored and quartered).

Clafoutis
(CHERRY CUSTARD PUDDING)

serves 6

800g/1¾lb ripe red or black cherries, washed and
  stalks removed
100g/3½oz/½cup flour
pinch of salt
200g/7oz/1cup caster sugar
3 large eggs
700ml/1¼pints/3cups milk
20ml/1tablespoon/1½tablespoons kirsch
butter for greasing

1 Sift the flour with a pinch of salt into a large
bowl. Stir in the sugar, reserving 3 tablespoons.
Work in the eggs, one at a time, beating them in
well with a wooden spoon.

2 Trickle in the milk, very slowly to begin with,
stirring well to prevent lumps forming. Flavour
with the kirsch.

3 Butter a large gratin dish. Arrange the cherries in
the dish, cover with the batter and bake for 40–45
minutes in a preheated 200°C/400°F/gas6 oven,
until set and golden.

4 Sprinkle with the
reserved sugar and
leave to cool a little
before serving.

Foire au Fromage de Chèvre

GOAT'S CHEESE FAIR

Goat's cheese is one of the *specialités* of the Loire and every year in early June cheese-makers from the region and further afield converge on Sainte-Maure in Touraine, a town famous for its fine-flavoured farmhouse cheeses. Competitors enter their cheese in the *concours*, the very tough, nationally famous championship, in the hope of winning the coveted gold trophy.

Salade au Fromage de Chèvre
(GOAT'S CHEESE SALAD)

serves 4
40ml/2tablespoons/3tablespoons olive oil
125g/4½oz moist goat's cheese
50ml/3tablespoons/¼cup grapeseed or
sunflower oil
20ml/1tablespoon/1½tablespoons red or white
  wine vinegar
250g/8½oz mixed salad leaves
several sprigs of flat-leaf parsley, finely chopped
croûtons, to serve
salt and freshly ground black pepper

1 In a frying-pan gently heat half the olive oil. Remove the crust from the cheese and cut into 8–12 small pieces. Sauté the cheese over a low heat until warm and lightly golden all over.

2 Pour the rest of the olive oil, the sunflower oil and the vinegar into the salad bowl. Stir well to blend, then season to taste with salt and pepper. Add the washed and dried salad leaves and parsley, and toss well. Place the sautéed cheese on top and serve at once with croûtons.

Croûtes au Fromage de Chèvre
(CHEESE CROUSTADES)

serves 4

100g/3½oz moist goat's cheese
20ml/1tablespoon/1½tablespoons cream or
    fromage frais
10ml/2teaspoons dry white wine
a few sprigs of chervil, finely chopped
4 slices of granary or other good bread, crusts
    removed
knob of butter
freshly ground black pepper

1 Using a fork, mash together the cheese, cream and wine. Season generously with pepper and mix in the herbs.
2 Lightly toast the bread on one side. Butter the untoasted side and spread the cheese mixture on top. Grill for a few minutes until bubbly and golden, and serve piping hot.

Pur Chèvre   9,5 oF

Foire à la Quiche Lorraine

BACON QUICHE FAIR

Perhaps less famous than neighbouring Alsace, the province of Lorraine in the north-east of the country has nevertheless given France many celebrated dishes and delicacies. Best known of all is the savoury bacon, cream and egg tart known as *Quiche Lorraine*. The dish has its own colourful fair every second year during the third weekend of June, in the small town of Dombasle-sur-Meurthe, not far from Nancy.

Quiche Lorraine
(BACON QUICHE)

serves 6
250g/8½oz shortcrust pastry
250g/8½oz thick cut rindless smoked streaky bacon
10ml/2teaspoons oil
30g/1oz butter, plus extra for greasing
3 large eggs
150ml/¼pint/⅔cup thick cream
ground nutmeg
salt and freshly ground black pepper

1 Roll out the pastry thinly and line a buttered 25cm/10in loose-bottomed tart tin, pressing it in lightly with your hands. Prick all over with a fork. Cover the pastry base with a piece of foil and dried beans, then bake in a preheated 190°C/375°F/gas5 oven for 15 minutes. Remove the foil and beans.
2 Meanwhile, blanch the bacon in boiling water. Drain well and pat dry with absorbent paper. Cut into small pieces.
3 Heat the oil in a frying-pan and sauté the bacon pieces until they are evenly crisp and golden. Drain well on absorbent paper.
4 Spread the bacon pieces over the pastry base. Arrange dots of butter in between the bacon pieces.
5 Beat together the eggs and cream. Season very lightly with salt (the bacon is salty) and nutmeg, and liberally with pepper. Pour the mixture into the pastry case and bake for about 20 minutes, until set and golden brown. (Pierce with a fork during baking if the filling swells unevenly.) Serve warm rather than piping hot.

La Saint-Jean

MIDSUMMER

Gone are the days when bonfires lit up the skies of the French countryside on the night of Midsummer. Alas people no longer believe that jumping over a fire will bring good luck or prevent warts... Yet around June 23rd many country fairs and traditional local festivities still celebrate the *Saint Jean* – the midsummer festival and the name day of St John the Baptist. The town of Uzès holds a garlic festival, at which, as at the many other garlic fairs that take place all over France throughout the summer, stacks and bundles of bulbs pile up on tables and barrows and cafés do a roaring trade. The air takes on a lightly pungent aroma – one that Alexandre Dumas thought was 'good for you to breathe'. In some villages the highlight of the occasion is the crowning of the Garlic Queen and the communal partaking of bowls of steaming garlic soup... Of the following dishes the one with the most intense garlic flavour is the *Aïoli*. For a gentler effect, blanch the cloves first as explained in the chicken recipe.

Soupe à l'Ail
(VEGETABLE AND GARLIC SOUP)

serves 6
20ml/1tablespoon/1½tablespoons olive oil
225g/8oz rindless smoked streaky bacon, chopped
450g/1lb each of carrots and potatoes, peeled and finely chopped
2 Spanish onions, finely chopped
250g/8½oz swedes or turnips, peeled and finely chopped
2 courgettes, chopped

4–6 garlic cloves, peeled and chopped
1.3litres/2¼pints/6cups warm chicken or vegetable
    stock, or a mixture of stock and water
few sprigs of thyme and marjoram
1–2 bay leaves
2 large tomatoes, coarsely chopped
1 small can flageolets or cannellini beans, drained
salt and freshly ground black pepper

To serve
garlic croûtons
freshly grated Parmesan,
    Gruyère or strong Cheddar

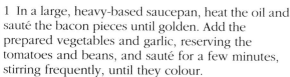

1 In a large, heavy-based saucepan, heat the oil and
sauté the bacon pieces until golden. Add the
prepared vegetables and garlic, reserving the
tomatoes and beans, and sauté for a few minutes,
stirring frequently, until they colour.
2 Pour in the stock, season lightly with salt and
pepper and add the herbs and bay leaves. Cover
and cook very gently for 1 hour.
3 Add the tomatoes and beans and cook for a
further 15 minutes.
4 Check the seasoning. Remove the sprigs of
herbs and bay leaves. Serve piping hot with garlic
croûtons and freshly grated cheese.

Aïoli

makes 500ml/16fl oz/2cups
1tablespoon/1½tablespoons stale breadcrumbs,
    moistened with milk and squeezed
4–6 garlic cloves, peeled and mashed
2 egg yolks at room temperature
400ml/⅔pint/1¾cups olive oil at room temperature
1tablespoon/1½tablespoons boiling water
a few drops of lemon juice
salt and freshly ground black pepper

To serve
a selection of cold cooked vegetables and
hard-boiled eggs
cold poached salt cod
leftover lamb or roast chicken

1 In a large bowl, combine the bread, mashed garlic
and egg yolks and season lightly with salt and
pepper.
2 Beat in the olive oil, a few drops at a time to
begin with, then in a thin trickle as for mayonnaise.
3 Once all the oil has been incorporated in the
aïoli, beat in the boiling water. Check the
seasoning and beat in a few drops of lemon juice
to taste. Cover with cling film and chill until ready
to use. Serve with cold cooked vegetables and
hardboiled eggs, fish, lamb or chicken.

Poulet Rôti à l'Ail
(ROAST CHICKEN WITH GARLIC)
This rich, golden chicken is good with French beans
and sautéed potatoes.

serves 4–6
1 oven-ready free-range or corn-fed chicken,
weighing approximately 2.3kg/4–5lbs
450g/1lb young garlic cloves
a few sprigs each of thyme, rosemary, marjoram
and/or oregano
40ml/2tablespoons/3tablespoons olive oil
30g/1oz butter
50ml/3tablespoons/¼cup dry white wine
50ml/3tablespoons/¼cup chicken stock
salt and freshly ground black pepper

1 Bring the chicken to room temperature.

2 Blanch the unpeeled garlic cloves in boiling water for 5–7minutes. Drain and plunge into cold water. Drain again. Squeeze each clove between your thumb and forefinger to peel off the skin.

3 Season the chicken inside and out with salt and pepper. Insert some of the herbs between the skin and the flesh and push the rest into the cavity. Put the chicken into a roasting dish. Tuck the prepared garlic under the bird and sprinkle with the olive oil. Dot with half the butter.

4 Roast the chicken for 40 minutes in a preheated 220°C/425°F/gas7 oven, basting and turning occasionally. Turn down the heat to 180°C/350°F/gas4 and continue roasting for a further 40 minutes or until cooked. Turn off the heat. Pour the cooking juices (but not the garlic) into a small pan and return the chicken and garlic to the oven.

5 Stir the wine and stock into the cooking juices and bring to a boil. Simmer the sauce for a few minutes until slightly reduced, then remove from the heat. Check the seasoning and stir in the rest of the butter.

6 Serve the chicken with the roasted garlic, and the sauce on the side.

Les Olivades

OLIVE FESTIVAL

The town of Nyons in the Drôme shares with Nice the honour of producing the best olives in France – small, firm and flavour packed. Every year in mid-July the olive festival, Les Olivades (from a provençal word meaning olive picking), solemnly opens with the resplendent Knights of the Olive Tree parading through the town.

The olive plays a vital part in the cooking of Provence. *Pan Bagna* – literally bathed bread – is the region's sunny version of the sandwich, and *Olives Cassées*, flavoured split olives, are traditionally nibbled with a glass of *pastis* or other apéritif.

Pan Bagna
(PROVENÇAL SANDWICH)

serves 2
2 large round bread rolls
1 garlic clove, peeled and halved
olive oil
2 ripe tomatoes (skinned and deseeded, if liked), thickly sliced
a few rings of mild white onion, or the white parts of 2 spring onions
8 black olives, stoned and coarsely chopped
2–4 basil leaves, finely chopped
2 sprigs of flat-leaf parsley, finely chopped
salt and freshly ground black pepper

1 Split the bread rolls and rub the insides with the cut sides of the garlic clove. Sprinkle generously with olive oil until the bread is well coated.

2 Fill with slices of tomato, rings of onion and olive pieces. Sprinkle with chopped basil and parsley. Season lightly with salt and pepper.

3 Wrap closely in a tea towel or kitchen paper and leave at room temperature for at least 30 minutes before eating.

Olives Cassées
(FLAVOURED SPLIT OLIVES)

300g/10½oz green olives
125g/4½oz sea salt
3 bay leaves
20ml/1tablespoon/1½tablespoons coarsely crushed
  coriander seeds
10ml/2teaspoons coarsely crushed fennel seeds
1litre/1¾pints/4½cups water
a couple of dried fennel stalks
olive oil, to serve

1 Bruise the olives with a small hammer or pestle without crushing them. Plunge them in plenty of cold water and leave to soak for 5 days, changing the water every day.

2 In a clean jar, combine the drained olives, salt, bay leaves, coriander and fennel seeds. Cover with the water and shake well. Top with the fennel stalks. Cover and leave to infuse for a week before using.

3 Drain well and sprinkle lightly with olive oil before serving.

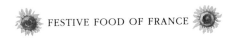

Fête des Pommiers

APPLE TREE FESTIVAL

Brittany has always been apple country. In the old days the twenty or so local varieties of apple were seldom eaten raw. For young people one of the highlights of the year was the *queiserie*, the big apple cook–up, when apples were slowly simmered with sweet cider in large cauldrons while dancing went on through the night and romance blossomed.

Bretons and visitors can still get a taste of traditional cider, cakes and music during the third week of July in Finistère, at the Fouesnant apple tree festival. The farmhouse cider competition on the Saturday is followed on Sunday by a colourful fair, with folkloric floats, traditional costumes and a fireworks display at night.

Gâteau Breton aux Pommes
(BRITTANY APPLE CAKE)

serves 8

Filling

450g/1lb Cox's orange pippin or Egremont russet
apples, peeled, cored and chopped

30g/1oz butter

1tablespoon/1½tablespoons sultanas

20ml/1tablespoon/1½tablespoons Calvados or
apple brandy

Cake

200g/7oz/1cup caster sugar

6 medium or 4 large egg yolks

200g/7oz/1cup butter, softened, plus extra for
greasing

20ml/1tablespoon/1½tablespoons Calvados

450g/1lb/4cups self-raising flour

20ml/1tablespoon/1½tablespoons milk, for glazing

1 To prepare the filling, melt the butter in a
saucepan, then stir in the prepared apples, sultanas
and Calvados. Cook over a low heat, stirring
occasionally, until the apples are soft.

2 Meanwhile, pour the sugar into a large bowl, and
whisk in the egg yolks, one at a time, until the
mixture is smooth and forms ribbons. Reserve a
little yolk for glazing. Work in the butter and the
Calvados, then sift in the flour, a little at a time.

3 Butter a deep, round loose-bottomed 20cm/8in
cake tin. Pour in half the cake mixture, spreading it
evenly with a spatula. Cover with the softened
apples. Top with the rest of the cake mixture and
smooth with a spatula. Combine the reserved yolk
with the milk and brush lightly over the cake.

4 Bake for about 45 minutes in a preheated 190°C/
375°F/gas5 oven, until cooked through and golden.
Remove from the tin and serve cold.

Pèlerinage de Notre-Dame du Rosaire

PILGRIMAGE OF OUR LADY OF THE ROSARY

Every year on September 8th the people of Bonifacio in Southern Corsica walk in pilgrimage to the Ermitage de la Trinité, a small convent a few kilometres from the town. After honouring Our Lady of the Rosary they traditionally eat a dish of stuffed aubergines, *Aubergines à la Bonifacienne*.

Aubergines Farcies à la Bonifacienne

(CORSICAN STUFFED AUBERGINES)

serves 4–6

3 even-sized plump unblemished large aubergines

60g/2oz/⅔cup 2-day-old breadcrumbs, soaked in a little milk and squeezed dry

2–3 garlic cloves, mashed

several leaves of fresh basil, finely chopped

2 medium eggs

15g/½oz butter, softened

45g/1½oz/¾cup freshly grated Parmesan

olive oil for frying

salt and freshly ground black pepper

Tomato Sauce

20ml/1tablespoon/1½tablespoons olive oil

½ mild Spanish onion, finely chopped

450g/1lb ripe tomatoes, blanched, peeled, deseeded and chopped

a pinch each of dried thyme and oregano

2 anchovy fillets, drained and mashed

salt and freshly ground black pepper

1 Cut the aubergines in half lengthways. Bring to the boil a large saucepan of lightly salted water. Add the aubergines and simmer them for 10 minutes, until part-cooked. Drain and leave to cool in a colander.

2 Meanwhile, prepare the tomato sauce. Heat the olive oil, add the onion and sauté over a low heat for a few minutes until softened, stirring frequently. Add the tomatoes, dried herbs and anchovy fillets. Cook gently until mushy, stirring occasionally. Liquidize and check the seasoning.

3 Squeeze the aubergines to extract as much water as possible. Scoop out the flesh, taking care not to pierce the skin. Squeeze the flesh again – it can never be too dry – then chop it finely. Reserve the shells, upside-down on a clean tea towel or absorbent paper.

4 In a bowl combine the prepared aubergine flesh, breadcrumbs, garlic and basil. Season generously with pepper, then work in the eggs, one at a time, and the butter. Stir in the grated Parmesan.

5 Spoon the filling into the aubergine shells.

6 In a large frying-pan heat a little olive oil. Starting with the filled side down, sauté the aubergines until cooked through and crispy brown. Add a little oil as necessary and keep the heat moderate. Serve hot, warm or cold with the tomato sauce.

45

Les Vendanges

THE WINE HARVEST

During late September and early October, when the days are still hot but a misty chill hangs over the mornings and evenings, sleepy villages all over France suddenly come to life, and buzz with activity and noise... This is wine harvest time, when the owners of the vineyards marshall their troops – family, friends, hired help from far and near – and deploy them among the rows of vines to pick the precious grapes. Timing is crucial, so the pace is fast and the work arduous, but the atmosphere is happy and convivial – especially if the crop is a good one.

Every meal is a feast with the boss's wife dispensing huge comforting stews to the hungry wine-harvesters. Stews vary with the regions, but one that is traditionally served, and not just in the area it is named after, is *Bœuf Bourguignon*, the great beef and red wine casserole of Burgundy. It is dished out without ceremony, straight from the pot, when the grape-pickers, *les vendangeurs*, come in from toiling in the vineyards. In Burgundy the beef simmers in the rich red local wine, preferably Hautes–Côtes de Beaune, but outside the province this may be replaced by a bottle of the most appropriate red the region has to offer.

The portions are generous, but wine harvest meals are simple. Only one plate is used for each guest, mopped clean of juices after each course with a piece of bread. A typical meal will start with a hot vegetable soup or tomato salad. *Bœuf Bourguignon* is invariably accompanied by mountains of boiled potatoes, and followed by a green salad, then local cheeses. The dessert tends to be fruit or an open fruit tart.

Bœuf Bourguignon
(BEEF AND RED WINE CASSEROLE)

serves 4–6

1kg/2¼lb lean stewing steak
3 thick rindless slices fatty smoked bacon
2 large Spanish onions
2 tablespoons/3 tablespoons flour
700ml/1¼pints/3 cups full-bodied red wine
bouquet garni
2 sage leaves
2 garlic cloves
18 button onions
30g/1oz butter
boiled or steamed potatoes, to serve
salt and freshly ground black pepper

1 Cut the beef into 5cm/2in cubes and chop up the bacon. Heat a heavy-based casserole and brown the bacon over a moderate heat.
2 Chop the Spanish onions, add them to the bacon and stir over the heat until golden. Remove the sautéed mixture with a slotted spoon and reserve.
3 Turn up the heat a little, add the beef to the pan and sauté the pieces until evenly browned. Sprinkle the meat with the flour and allow to colour for a minute or two.
4 Pour in the wine. Add the bouquet garni, sage leaves and whole cloves of garlic. Season to taste with salt and pepper. Return the bacon and onion mixture to the casserole. Cover tightly and simmer very gently for 1¾hours, stirring once or twice.
5 Meanwhile, peel the button onions, then heat the butter in a small frying-pan and the sauté the onions until golden.
6 Add the onions to the casserole, stir, cover again and continue cooking for another ¾ hour.
7 Serve the stew piping hot from the casserole with boiled or steamed potatoes.

La Toussaint

ALL SAINTS' DAY

November 1st, All Saints, is a public holiday in
France. It is the eve of *Le Jour des Morts*, All Souls,
and the time when the dead are remembered.
Village church bells used to toll all night while
people held a wake and said prayers. They
sustained themselves seasonally with freshly picked
chestnuts and the first of the harvest's young wines.
Customs and superstitions varied from region to
region, but there was a widely held belief that for
each chestnut you roasted in the fire and ate, a
soul was saved from purgatory.

Chestnuts have always been an important
foodstuff in France, particularly in the southern half
of the country, where their trees were once known
as 'bread trees'. Innumerable chestnut fairs still take
place in the autumn in the run-up to the *Toussaint*.
The soup recipe below comes from the Limousin
where it was typical rural fare.

Soupe aux Châtaignes

(CHESTNUT SOUP)

serves 6
400g/14oz large chestnuts
5ml/1teaspoon oil
1.5litres/2½pints/6¼cups water
2 Spanish onions, coarsely chopped
2 leeks, trimmed, washed and sliced
1 large waxy potato, peeled and chopped
125ml/4½fl oz/⅔cup single cream
30g/1oz butter
salt and freshly ground black pepper

1 Nick the shells of the chestnuts with a sharp knife. Put them in a large saucepan with a pinch of salt and the oil. Cover with water and bring to the boil, then simmer for 10 minutes. Drain the chestnuts and remove the shells and inner skin as soon as they are cool enough to handle.

2 Rinse the pan. Pour in the water and add the prepared chestnuts and vegetables. Season with a little salt and pepper, then slowly bring to the boil and simmer gently for 40 minutes, or until the chestnuts and vegetables are cooked.

3 Pass the chestnuts and vegetables through a mouli, or liquidize with a little of the liquid. Return the purée to the pan and stir into the liquid.

4 Stir in the cream and heat through gently, without letting the soup come to the boil. Check the seasoning, swirl in the butter, and serve at once.

La Saint-Martin

THE FEAST OF ST MARTIN

Hundreds of French villages and thousands of churches are named after St Martin, the dashing Roman soldier who, legend has it, once gave half his cloak to a shivering beggar. His feast on November 11th is now somewhat obscured by the fact that this is also a public holiday commemorating the end of World War I.

In the north and north-east of the country in particular, banquets honouring the saint invariably feature a goose as a *pièce de résistance*. They are also a perfectly timed opportunity to taste the season's new wines. This Martinmas goose pot-roast comes from the Lorraine.

Oie en Daube de la Saint-Martin
(GOOSE POT-ROAST)

serves 6
1 small goose, jointed
100g/3½oz rindless smoked streaky bacon, chopped
30g/1oz/¼cup flour
500ml/16fl oz/2cups dry white wine
2 bay leaves
a few sprigs each of parsley and thyme
1 large ripe tomato, blanched, peeled, deseeded and chopped
40g/1½oz butter
18 button onions, peeled and blanched
5ml/1teaspoon sugar
2 shallots, finely chopped
1 garlic clove, finely chopped
3tablespoons finely chopped flat-leaf parsley
salt and freshly ground black pepper

1 Heat a large heavy-based saucepan or casserole dish and sauté the bacon until crisp. Add the jointed goose and sauté until browned, turning the pieces over a few times. Pour off the fat.

2 Sprinkle with the flour, stir for a minute, then pour in the wine and top with enough water to just cover the pieces of goose. Add the bay leaves, herbs and chopped tomato. Season lightly with salt and pepper. Cover tightly and simmer gently over a low heat for a good two hours. Stir once after the first hour.

3 In a frying-pan, melt the butter over a moderate heat. Once it is hot, add the onions to the pan, sprinkle them with sugar and sauté them until they turn an even golden brown.

4 Stir the onions into the pot-roast and continue cooking, uncovered, for 10–15 minutes.

5 Combine the finely chopped shallots, garlic and parsley in a small bowl.

6 Remove the bay leaves and sprigs of herbs from the pot-roast and check the seasoning. Sprinkle with the shallot mixture and serve at once.

Saint Nicolas

ST NICHOLAS

On the night of December 5th, the eve of the feast of Saint Nicholas, young children in north and north-east France are unusually well-behaved. Before going to bed they put out their shoes and some straw in front of the chimney, for their patron saint and for the donkey he always rides on his travels. In return for this kind attention, Saint Nicholas traditionally leaves behind spiced biscuits shaped in his own image.

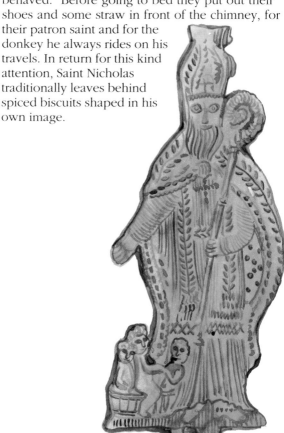

Pain d'Epice

SPICED BISCUITS

makes 14–20, depending on size

125g/4½oz/⅓cup runny honey
125g/4½oz/⅓cup molasses
75g/2½oz/⅓cup caster sugar
5ml/1teaspoon vanilla essence
125g/4½oz/½cup butter
1 large egg
400g/14oz/3½cups wholemeal flour
10ml/2teaspoons baking powder
pinch of salt
100g/3½oz/½cup ground almonds
finely grated zest of 1 lemon and 1 orange
10ml/2teaspoons ground cinnamon
5ml/1teaspoon ground nutmeg
5ml/1teaspoon aniseed

Glaze
75ml/5tablespoons/⅓cup orange juice
7–8 tablespoons icing sugar

1 Combine the honey, molasses, caster sugar and vanilla essence in a saucepan. Heat gently until dissolved, then stir in the butter until melted. Leave to cool.
2 Work in the egg, flour and then the remaining ingredients. Mix into a dough, then cover and leave to rest overnight in a cool place.
3 Roll out the dough to about 1cm/½in thick. Using biscuit cutters, cut the dough into gingerbread men or heart shapes. Arrange the dough shapes on greased baking sheets and bake for 10–15 minutes in a preheated 200°C/400°F/gas6 oven until golden and just firm to the touch.
4 Remove from the oven. Make a glaze by combining the orange juice and icing sugar. Brush over the biscuits while they are still warm. Transfer to a rack with a palette knife and leave to cool.

Noël

CHRISTMAS

Christmas in France has always been both a religious and a family feast. In the old days the most significant, religious part of the celebrations took place on Christmas Eve, when the whole family would gather together for supper and to go to Midnight Mass. This was a happy reunion and friends and family would gather round the hearth and sing and tell stories. In keeping with the religious significance of the evening, the dishes shared were fairly simple – soups, breads, cakes, vegetables. Fish and snails were allowed but no meat was served. *Aligot*, eaten on Christmas Eve in the Auvergne, is made with the potatoes and cheese that are local everyday fare.

After the relative abstinence of Christmas Eve, large and elaborate meat courses were joyfully consumed the following day. People feasted on the region's most sumptuous dishes. The stuffed chicken recipe on the following pages comes from Gascony.

Aligot
(POTATO AND CHEESE PUREE)

serves 4–6
900g/2lb waxy potatoes
75g/2½oz/⅓cup butter
75ml/5tablespoons/⅓cup milk
100ml/4fl oz/½cup *crème fraîche* or thick cream
350g/12oz *tomme d'aligot* or young farmhouse
   Lancashire or Caerphilly, finely slivered
2 garlic cloves, finely chopped
20ml/1tablespoon/1½tablespoons good bacon fat
   (optional)
salt and freshly ground black pepper

1 Bring plenty of lightly salted water to the boil in a
large heavy-based saucepan. Add the potatoes,
reduce the heat and simmer gently until the
potatoes are soft but not disintegrating. Drain
carefully, then peel the potatoes as soon as they
are cool enough to handle.
2 Melt the butter in the pan over a low heat. Pass
the potatoes through a mouli, or mash them lightly
but thoroughly. Stir them into the melted butter,
then add the milk and cream and stir until
combined.
3 Work the slivered cheese into the purée a little
at a time, using a wooden spoon. Mix in the garlic,
and the bacon fat if using. Season generously with
pepper.
4 Continue stirring over a low heat for a good 5
minutes, until the cheese starts to make strings.
Serve at once.

La Poule au Pot Farcie
STUFFED CHICKEN

serves 12

1 very large corn-fed chicken, weighing
approximately 2.3kg/5lb
4 large waxy potatoes, peeled and quartered
4 large leeks, trimmed, washed, and cut into thick
segments

For the boiled beef
1 large marrow bone
550g/1¼lb lean braising steak, trimmed of visible
fat, cut into 5cm/2in pieces
550g/1¼lb shin of beef, cut into 5cm/2in pieces
3 garlic cloves, peeled and halved
3 bay leaves
several sprigs of thyme
4 large carrots, peeled and cut into segments
4 medium turnips, trimmed, peeled and quartered
1 Spanish onion, studded with cloves
12 button onions, peeled
3 celery stalks, washed, trimmed and cut into
segments
salt and freshly ground black pepper

For the chicken stuffing
150g/5½oz rindless dry-cured smoked ham
100g/3½oz day-old breadcrumbs, soaked in a little
milk and squeezed
giblets from the chicken
75g/2½oz veal escalope
1 garlic clove
3 shallots
3tablespoons finely chopped parsley
2 medium eggs
salt and freshly ground black pepper

To serve
Tomato sauce (page 44–5)
mustard
strongly flavoured mayonnaise

gherkins
coarse sea salt

1 First prepare the boiled beef. In a stockpot large enough to take the meat *and* chicken, cover the marrow bone and meat with plenty of water, then add the garlic, bay leaves and thyme. Bring to the boil very slowly, skimming any grey scum that comes up.

2 Add the prepared vegetables and bring back to a gentle boil. Skim and season lightly with salt and pepper.

3 Meanwhile, prepare the stuffing for the chicken. Finely mince together or process all the ingredients. Stir in the eggs and season. Spoon the stuffing into the cavity and sew it up with a trussing needle and fine string, then truss the chicken with the string.

4 Place the chicken on top of the beef and vegetables. Cover and cook slowly for 2–2½hours, skimming occasionally. Add the potatoes and leeks after one hour.

5 To serve, lift out the chicken and the beef with a slotted spoon. Arrange the beef on a large dish, reserving the marrow bone. Remove the strings from the chicken and place on top of the beef. Surround with the vegetables, discarding the onion studded with cloves, bay leaves and sprigs of thyme. Spoon out the marrow and dot it over the vegetables (or give it on a piece of toast to your most senior guest).

6 Check the seasoning of the stock. Strain through a fine sieve into a jug, reserving a little to moisten the meats and vegetables. Serve at once, with the jug of stock and the accompaniments.

57

Les Treize Desserts
(THIRTEEN CHRISTMAS SWEETS)

On Christmas Eve in Provence, families traditionally sat round a table laid with three white cloths, lit with three candles, for a ritual supper, *le gros souper*.

The meal was washed down with *vin cuit*, mulled wine, and ended with a magnificent spread of sweets and desserts – thirteen in all to represent Christ and his disciples – including dried and fresh fruits, almonds and walnuts, roast chestnuts, raisins, dates and prunes filled with marzipan, jams, quince paste (see recipe). Though the foods varied from village to village, always included were honeyed nougats, black or white, flavoured with pistachio or studded with pinenuts, and a sweet flavoured bread called *Pompe*.

Pompe
(PROVENÇAL CHRISTMAS BREAD)

serves6

250g/8½oz bread dough
40ml/2tablespoons/3tablespoons olive oil, plus
  extra for greasing
grated zest of 1 lemon and 1 orange
10ml/2teaspoons ground aniseed
85g/3oz/⅓cup caster sugar
2 medium eggs

1 Work into the bread dough the remaining ingredients, reserving a little egg yolk for glazing, mixed with 1tablespoon water in a small cup.
2 Roll out the dough into a circle about 2cm/¾in thick. Slit with a knife at regular intervals. Leave to rest in a warm place for a few hours.
3 Brush the dough lightly with egg glaze. Place on a greased baking sheet and bake in a preheated

190°C/375°F/gas5 oven for about 20 minutes, until cooked and golden. Serve warm or cold, with hot mulled wine.

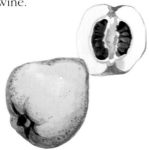

Pâte de Coings
(QUINCE PASTE)

makes 1.8kg/4lb
1kg/2¼lb unpeeled ripe quinces, quartered
125ml/4½fl oz/⅔cup water
5ml/1 teaspoon ground nutmeg
2 cloves
caster sugar

1 In a large saucepan, boil the quinces with the water, nutmeg and cloves until soft. Strain, discarding the cores and cloves. Purée, then weigh the pulp.
2 Pour the pulp into a clean saucepan. Add the same weight of caster sugar and cook gently for 30 minutes, stirring very frequently. The paste is cooked when it slides off a spoon in one piece. Pour into a tin and leave to get cold.
3 To serve, turn the paste out of the tin. Cut it into small circles, squares and lozenges and roll lightly in sugar. The paste keeps well if wrapped and chilled.

Le Réveillon de la Saint-Sylvestre et le Jour de l'An

NEW YEAR'S EVE AND NEW YEAR'S DAY

Whereas Christmas remains a genuine *fête de famille*, a decorous family celebration, New Year's Eve and New Year's Day have become an extravaganza of feasting. Of the rituals associated with the end of the old year and the start of the new, all that remain are decorative bunches of mistletoe. People spend their time at the table indulging in fine foods and wines. Oysters, foie gras, lobsters, champagne... no expense is spared.

Restaurants put up their prices and offer special menus – sometimes very special indeed. In the besieged, starving Paris of 1870, diners at the luxurious Chez Peter's had to make do with elephant escalopes and roasted bear supplied by the Zoo. A generation or so later, a more orthodox *Réveillon* menu featured a bisque of langoustine, turbot, pheasant soufflé, guinea fowl in curried sauce, a gratin of cardoons, orange fritters and a pineapple charlotte topped with pistachio zabaglione. *Bon appétit!*

Filets de Turbot au Champagne

(TURBOT WITH A CHAMPAGNE SAUCE)

serves 4

4 skinned turbot fillets, no less than 200g/7oz each
20ml/1tablespoon/1½tablespoons oil
100g/3½oz/½cup butter
3 shallots, finely chopped
115g/4oz button mushrooms, rinsed, patted dry
  and thinly sliced
20ml/1tablespoon/1½tablespoons chopped parsley
20ml/1tablespoon/1½tablespoons flour
100ml/4fl oz/½cup reduced fish stock boiled down
  from 200ml/7fl oz/¾cup
175ml/6fl oz/¾cup champagne or dry sparkling
  wine
150ml/¼pint/⅔cup thick cream
salt and white pepper

1 Heat the oil and a third of the butter in a heavy-based pan large enough to take the turbot fillets side by side. Over a low heat sauté the shallots for a few minutes, then stir in the prepared mushrooms and parsley and sauté until tender. Remove from the pan with a fish slice.
2 Season the flour with a small pinch of salt and a little pepper. Lightly dust the turbot fillets with the seasoned flour. Add half the remaining butter to the pan and carefully sauté the turbot fillets until lightly coloured on both sides.
3 Return the shallot mixture to the pan, with the reduced fish stock and half the champagne. Simmer very gently for a few minutes, then lift the fillets onto a heated serving dish. Keep warm.
4 Add the cream to the cooking liquid and stir over a low heat until hot. Stir in the remaining champagne, heat through and check the seasoning.
5 Swirl in the rest of the butter, stir, then pour over the turbot fillets. Serve at once.